For Nan: Thank you for standing by me and
supporting me with such amazingly loving patience.
And for Abe, Bre, Ali, and Kelsie: You each
light up my world brighter than you can
possibly know.

Contents

Introduction

"I DON'T KNOW! I'LL TRY. HELP! PLEASE HELP!" I shouted panicking.

"Try to make it to your front door and stay on the line, the ambulance is on its way."

"OK," I said, as I slumped off the bed and crawled toward the door.

I managed to pull the sliding door open from my knees amid moans of "OW! OW! HELP! HELP!" All I could think to do was keep yelling and begging for help. Nan immediately woke up to my screams and rushed into the kitchen. Horror painted her face as she saw my skeletal naked frame screaming in agony crawling across the floor. Moments later a knock rapped on the door...it could have only been a few minutes from when I made the call.

"What happened? What's going on??" she demanded. The front door swung open as freezing winter mountain air rushed in with four EMT's.

"I DON'T KNOW! I DON'T KNOW!" I shouted in loud monotone.

"BLANKET! BLANKET!!" More shouting. "WATER! I NEED WATER! IT'S GONNA BLOW! IT'S GONNA BLOW UP!!! BLANKET!!"

"What's gonna blow?" she asked. "What's wrong??"

"I DON'T KNOW! MY GROIN! I DON'T KNOW!" Fiercely shivering now and still screaming, they loaded me onto a stretcher and asked for my name and birth date. Explosive pain

1

threatened to burst me to pieces. They piled three blankets over me and I rolled out the door and into the waiting ambulance. More questions as they strapped me into place: "What's your name?" "Aaron Kennard!" I replied. "What's your date of birth?" they asked. "Didn't they already ask me that two times in the house?" I wondered. I told them again. "They must be testing to see if I'm coherent. Yes, I'm here! And I'm exploding!! Please help me!!" My mind raced.

One EMT sprayed a pain drug into my nose. No relief. Then the ambulance flew down the road with sirens blaring. "Please God, let me live! I don't want to die. Please help me!!" were my thoughts. From my mouth came "OW!! OW! AM I GOING TO DIE?"

Nothing like any pain I had ever experienced, I had the distinct feeling death was imminent. I didn't fear dying for my own sake. But thoughts of my wife and children's well-being consumed me and I deeply yearned to stay alive for their sake. The thought of leaving Nan alone with our four little kids simply unbearable. Overwhelmed, I could only keep asking, "AM I GOING TO DIE? PLEASE HELP ME!"

In the living room at home, broken and dejected on her knees, Nan sobbed uncontrollably. "Please, Heavenly Father! Please don't let him die! Please let him be OK!!! PLEASE!!"

Why Are We Here?

Not like 'on this earth', silly, I mean why are you and I here together right now via this book?

Our Freedom! This book contains experiences from a year of my life, and some lessons learned. I'm sharing it with you now for one purpose: To give you the gift of freedom.

Freedom, from what? Aren't you already free?!

Well, yes and no. You may live in a free country, and even if you don't, you are absolutely free to think for yourself.

But I want to give you the gift of *freedom from yourself.* I want to free you from limiting thought habits and beliefs that are binding you down and holding you apart from the vast, limitless, abundance of joy that you should be and could be experiencing right now. And if you don't think you have any 'limiting beliefs'…well…I'll put it nicely, the fact is you do. We all do. And every moment that we are unwilling to be teachable, correctable, and open to rooting out limiting beliefs and changing them is a moment we are binding ourselves down and holding ourselves apart from our true potential; the potential of unimaginable joy and happiness.

When you finish reading this book you will feel empowered, hopeful, and optimistic. You will feel freer, more alive, and more faithful. You will feel more joy and you will know how to never have a bad day ever again.

That is my promise to you. And if you don't feel and know those things and your life and existence hasn't improved after reading this book, then I have failed and you deserve a full refund. And if I gave you this for free, well…I guess I'm in debt then right? I don't believe that will happen though.

But why should you listen to me? How can I be making such bold promises?

Simply put, I'm a happy person who has learned to find joy in easy times as well as extremely hard times. Many people can't seem to find consistent joy in any times, and are constantly trying to find joy in *stuff*...which is a futile and endless task. And many more find it easy to be full of joy when everything is going according to their plans, but find it impossible to feel joy when things don't seem to be working out as well, or they are confronted with major pain, illness, or any number of emotional challenges in life.

I have had the blessing of going through some of the most painful circumstances imaginable, and have witnessed personally that it is possible to experience joy regardless of any of it.

Joy is our purpose of existence. Yet pain in life is inevitable. Doesn't that make our purpose impossible at times then? Actually no, not when you learn to find joy even in pain. I love this interaction between Wesley and Princess Buttercup in "The Princess Bride" when Wesley tested her faithfulness to him: "You mock my pain!" she said. "Life is pain, highness! Anyone who says differently is selling something."

There is a lot of truth and beauty in that. How could we experience true joy without knowing its contrast? Pain and adversity are wonderful blessings to us, if seen from the lens of knowing they are absolutely essential to our receiving a fullness of joy in this life and beyond.

By reading my experiences, my hope is that you will be enabled to experience immense joy regardless of the circumstances you face in your own life. I hope you will be capable of embracing all your experiences, and seeing the goodness, beauty, and perfection in all of it; the seemingly good and bad. It is wise to remember that things aren't always what they seem.

So onward, shall we? Come with me now and let us discover the Positive Thinking Secret. Let's find out how to experience immense joy regardless of extreme highs or extreme lows. 2012 for me was a thrilling and also terrifying ride, and makes for a great case study in our quest to abolish the bad day, cast it out of our lives forever, and make every day amazing.

Chapter 1

A Year of Extremes

Lukewarm

From a bland, mediocre existence, to a thrilling flight through clouds of happy bliss, to an agonizing crawl through the valley of the shadow of death, the 2012 rollercoaster of life did not disappoint!

As I rode high on easy happiness the first half of the year, I came to the strong conclusion that this is a truly amazing life. Then that conclusion suffered severe testing and I questioned it many times. But the theory withstood the test, and I have come to believe stronger than ever that it's true.

Life was just lukewarm in 2011 for me though, which is an insidious state. In many ways I was just 'getting by': passionate about my family and my running hobby, but becoming bored out of my mind in my work.

In the early years, my real estate business excited me. But now 5 years in, I found myself consistently telling people that it was boring...going through the motions BIG TIME at work, getting it done because it had to be done, but constantly looking forward to the evening, or the weekend.

Don't get me wrong, I thought life was pretty good. Business was good and we had plenty of money. I had tons of awesome things to look forward to, and I was happy a lot of the time...mostly when I wasn't at work though. I really enjoyed running and super fun adventures with my wife and three amazing children. Life was pretty great in general.

But my life lacked the fulfillment, excitement, or thrill that it had once had. I was not in love with all of my life. I felt disturbed and frustrated in work, and didn't feel much closer to my goals than I had when I started. I saw that I had been running on a hamster wheel as hard as possible for five years and found myself near the same place I started. So half of my life rocked! But a huge part of it, my work, needed some serious help.

A Tipping Point

In November 2011 I got a sore throat that lasted for 4 weeks. In the 3rd week of annoying and relentless throat pain, and after seeing two doctors who found no solution, I had an experience that changed the way I viewed everything in my life.

One night during the usual stabbing pain each time I swallowed, I wondered, frustrated and annoyed, how I would get to sleep with the nuisance. Then an idea popped into my head: "Next time it hurts, think of 5 or 10 things you're grateful for."

I did it, and felt an instant lift of my emotions. Then I swallowed and felt the intense pain in my throat again. So I thought of five or six more things I felt super grateful for. This time, I began feeling happy as I thought of my amazing wife, my three children, and many other wonderful things in my life. Then I swallowed again. The pain was there, but I didn't mind as much. I started to feel great and to really enjoy the feeling. Feelings of stark contrast to the overwhelmment, annoyance, and lethargy that I felt as I laid down.

"How is this pain in my throat going to benefit me?"

I had been asking that daily for 3 weeks. I had come to believe that all adversity carries the seed of an equivalent advantage. "Where is the advantage to this?" I continually asked.

And in that moment in bed that night, the truth of that principle planted itself deep within my core as I realized that as long as this pain was here, it would serve me. I would make it a reminder to express gratitude in my thoughts. By deciding to use the pain in that way it would actually assist me in feeling immense joy emotionally.

Completely Empowered By Pain

As I realized that, I felt extremely empowered and my emotions soared. The next time I swallowed and felt the pain, my first thought was "Thank you for this sore throat!!" And I deeply meant it and it felt amazing to think it. I truly felt grateful for the experience with the pain right in that moment. And I witnessed that I had learned an immensely valuable lesson that I could not have learned without that experience of pain.

I slept in peace that night, and I woke up on cloud nine the next day. I felt so excited about life all of a sudden, and so empowered by what I could do with pain as a reminder, that I was totally OK if the sore throat stayed or went away. I now knew that either way, I would experience joy, and no amount of pain was going to stop me (at least I thought so at the time).

That moment in bed instilled in me the deep and personal knowledge that *my circumstances do not dictate my happiness or joy.*

I then knew on a deep internal level that there really is potential goodness in all things that show up in my life. And that I can find it. I then believed more firmly than ever that *everything is conspiring for our benefit.*

That day, life became truly amazing and a wonder to me. And every single day for over eight months afterward I woke up full of gratitude and excitement for life, absolutely thrilled to be alive. Previously I had good days and bad days like most people. And I really didn't think there was anything I could do to fully control that.

That day everything changed...

Stop Settling And Start Living

That became one of my mantras since that fateful night in December 2011. And I can honestly say that I have not had any bad days since then, which is hard to believe for most people when I tell them. But I have learned how it is possible to never have a bad day.

Now wait a minute! Before you go thinking I'm totally full of it, since I already told you about an ambulance hauling me off with exploding guts, I will tell you that I absolutely did not consider that a bad day either. Am I crazy? Perhaps. You can be the judge. But it is true. I have not had a bad day since December 2011. And I'm convinced stronger than ever that it is absolutely possible to never have a bad day ever again. And I will show you what I mean soon.

As 2012 progressed I found myself completely thrilled to wake up each morning. I had finally figured out how to live a fully joyful life and to stop settling for mediocre. Things that discouraged me at work before were suddenly no problem. In fact I started seeing everything in an entirely new light. And that changed everything. My heart filled with gratitude when my head hit the pillow at night, and spilled to overflowing every morning. I had somehow broken into a place in life where everything felt magical...and it was largely due to simple gratitude.

To live in a constant state of gratitude is to live in joy. Even challenges and trials don't stop you from experiencing joy when you are in a state of awe and gratitude for everything in life. In fact they only serve to deepen your joy.

I wrote this in my journal one afternoon as I pondered a discussion I had with a friend:

Life is good…and that is a true tragedy!

Because life has the constant potential to be Amazing, to settle for 'good' is to sacrifice Amazing. And that is tragic.

"Life is good…I can't stand my job, but things are good at home, and my job gives me a steady income, so I guess things aren't so bad."

That is called settling.

My friend said that to me today, and I wished there was something I could do to help him see the Amazing Life that is eagerly awaiting him the moment he opens his heart and mind to it.

It has been said "Good is the enemy to Great.". I would add that even great, if it doesn't encompass one's entire existence, is the enemy to Amazing.

I believe This Is A Truly Amazing Life. And it deserves to be lived for what it is.

I don't believe we came to this earth to see if we could figure out how to have a pretty good existence. I don't believe it is compatible with our true nature, to waste even one moment settling for a second-rate, miserable experience in any aspect of our lives.

I believe each person on this planet is equally endowed with freedom to choose and a divine connection to infinite intelligence. I believe that all people are truly amazing at the core, but many do not remember that yet, so, many of us are not enjoying the fullness of our divine privilege and birthright.

To say "I hate my job," or "I'm bored with my work, but I'm going to keep plugging away, getting by, because it pays the bills," is no different than saying, "I don't believe I deserve an Amazing Life. It is how life is supposed to be that we are only happy with some aspects of it. I'm OK with just feeling good occasionally, life was not meant to be that great anyway. Maybe if I just stick it out at this crappy job that I hate for another few years, then somehow a great job that I love will come along. Then I'll be truly happy."

Those are all just a bunch of lies though.

We are ALL so much more deserving, amazing, genius and capable than any of us can even begin to fathom. We come directly from God. We are part of the infinite intelligence of the universe. We are connected to it, and we are never separated from it. And we cannot even comprehend the magnitude of the power, strength, genius, goodness and love that we are inherently part of.

So why not forget about 'good' entirely and look only at Amazing? To me, anything less, is not who I am, and it's not acceptable to me. In my view, settling for less than who God created me to be is the biggest tragedy ever.

Instead of settling, let's accept the truth of who we are – absolutely amazing beings fully deserving of a Truly Amazing Life – and let's live for that!

Let's go to what used to be our "boring" or "annoying" or "frustrating" jobs or businesses or relationships with a completely different set of eyes. Let's go there knowing we will find the good today. Let's go forward with pure gratitude in our hearts for the opportunities right in our face. Let's decide to love all aspects of our life, and pour out our soul in love and service wherever we are.

We don't need a new job or anything else to experience a full, passionate, amazing life. We simply need to change the way we look at things, and the things we look at will change.

To choose to see your entire life as Truly Amazing, is to make it so.

I had somehow learned how to be truly grateful; how to never settle. And it was magnificent! But how did it happen? I asked myself that a lot.

Why?

In the early spring I pondered and wrote for many weeks about what it was that was bringing me so much joy. And why I woke up so thrilled with each new day now. And why all my circumstances improved so dramatically and suddenly. I felt drawn to creating a crystal clear written reminder to myself of what was causing all this new found joy and enthusiasm for life, in the event that something happened to pull me off track or make me forget in the future.

On a flight to Boston (to run my first official marathon in April) I wrote page after page the entire flight, asking the question "Why?" Every time I wrote an answer, I asked the question again of that answer. I kept digging and digging and just dumping every thought that popped into my head onto paper. I couldn't believe we were landing a few hours later; it felt like 30 minutes.

The result I came up with was this poster that I created in Photoshop and had printed and framed on my wall. (See page 201 for more detailed view or to print your own copy free go to TrulyAmazingLife.com/tal-poster)

This poster is my 'why'. It contains the reasons I exist. Living these principles is what I discovered to be the root of my joy and fulfillment. And you'll notice that 'have millions of dollars' or 'have the perfect body' didn't make the list. Those things are great, but living a truly amazing life has little to do with material possessions and everything to do with your heart and mind and the decisions you make.

I came to realize that every single aspect of my life lined up with these words, and that is why I felt so good and so happy all the time. And from then on I wanted to keep it that way!

I realized that if something I thought or said didn't line up with the ideas on this poster, then it had no place in my life. Because living a Truly Amazing Life means to stop settling for less than I want in any area. It means, among other things, that I create the life I want and there is never a good reason to settle for less. It means living life full of awe, wonder, and amazement at the beauty of it all, and focusing on serving and giving love.

So I created this poster as a reminder for myself. In case I find myself settling again and telling myself that life is just OK. If I find myself thinking again there are good days and bad days, then I just need to look over at this poster and it will remind me of the beliefs that actually serve me. I created it for a foundation. As an anchor to keep me from drifting away when future storms would surely come. As a tool to keep my mind focused on what I want most and more importantly why I want it.

And I encourage you to do something similar. I encourage anyone who will listen, to look themselves in the eye and sincerely ask themselves, "Why am I alive?" And be completely open and brutally honest, and then write it all down. Then clarify it and keep it close as a reminder. Seek to understand what truly motivates you at the deepest level possible, and what it's all about for you. And once you know yourself at that level, make some way to remind yourself of your true self, because time and life will tend to make you forget. **But if you can remember who you truly are, you will live in a state of joy, peace and fulfillment that is indescribable.**

After creating the poster I realized that these answers to my questions are universal and apply to everyone. I believe anyone who lives the principles on this poster will be fulfilled and joyful. What I have found personally, and seen and heard from hundreds of others, is that loving, giving and constantly growing is where true fulfillment is found.

===============

Note: We have made the 18x24" version of this poster available for purchase online at:

TrulyAmazingLife.com/tal-poster

Little did I know when I made the poster however, that just a few months down the road it would help pull me through the most painful experiences I could possibly imagine. Something inside deeply motivated me to make it as a reminder for myself, for reasons I couldn't know at the time. And I'm so glad that I did.

Everything Happens For Your Good

That spring continued to be an amazing and blissful time of growth and expansion. Here's a journal entry from May 6, 2012, written after I read this scripture one morning:

> *"The natural man is an enemy to God, and has been since the fall of Adam, and will be, forever and ever, unless he yields to the enticings of the Holy Spirit. And putteth off the natural man and becometh a saint through the atonement of Christ the Lord, and becometh as a child, meek submissive, humble, patient, full of love, willing to **submit to all things which the Lord seeth fit to inflict upon him**, even as a child doth submit to his father." Mosiah 3:19, Book of Mormon*

> *The point for me is this: All things that happen to us are from God and are for our good. Our job is to submit ourselves to God's will.*

> *This is so simple! It doesn't need to be hard. Simply accept, believe, and know – without doubt or hesitation – that ALL things are blessing you, teaching you, and benefiting you. God is stretching out his hand all the day long. It is only when we try to separate ourselves that we suffer. But as we submit humbly, willingly, full of faith - and even cheerfully - to everything that God sees fit to place in*

our experience, then we find consistent joy, fulfillment, peace, and progress.

I knew that to be true and it had radically altered my state of living. And I began spending as much time as possible figuring out ways to help others discover a similar state.

By this time I had been able outsource or delegate most of the project management duties in my real estate business. I enjoy real estate. I like the process of buying a house that is beat up and transforming it into something beautiful for people to enjoy. I also enjoy the freedom of running my own business, deciding my own schedule, and living on my own terms every day. But I felt drawn toward freeing up my time to spend more of it each day pursuing things I felt would make a much bigger impact in people's lives. I had a feeling I was not living up to my full potential. That I was capable of giving much more to the world through writing and teaching and it was time to start giving it.

Life was really, really good. I could not help smiling...a lot. Pretty much all of the time, in fact. To the point that some people even mentioned to my wife that they were annoyed with how happy and positive I always seemed to be, while they were feeling discouraged or down. I certainly didn't try to annoy anyone! But I think I can understand where they were coming from...sometimes it's hard to see other people so happy when you feel so down yourself. And I was learning that sometimes perhaps I might need to tone down the enthusiasm in order to be more considerate of others when I notice they are not feeling great.

Is that true? I'm not really sure actually. What is the best way to help someone who is down and discouraged? Get down and discouraged with them? I don't think that's it. But I can also see how just bouncing off the walls with enthusiasm and big grins because life is so amazing may not help them much either. My gut tells me it's somewhere in between. That being empathetic and simply listening with an understanding ear is likely the best thing to do. I wrestled with this quite a bit through the first half of 2012. Many days my wife struggled with severe sickness in her first trimester of pregnancy with our fourth child. I looked for ways to reconcile feeling so fantastic personally, while watching her suffering and feeling miserable.

What I found was that staying happy and remaining in a place of love was the best thing I could do for her. I could see no benefit to me getting miserable with her. I just had to love her, and trust and know this too would pass and she would feel better soon. It wouldn't do me any good to feel guilty about feeling happy within myself while she was feeling sad.

But it was hard to tone down because I felt so fantastic!

One morning while writing I felt like describing in vivid detail what an amazing way to live life would look and feel like:

May 17, 2012 – A journal entry

Imagine an existence where you open your eyes in the morning and immediately as you glance around, you are flooded with thoughts of gratitude for the abundance in your life. And your heart fills with joyful feelings as you think of dozens of things you are overcome with gratitude for.

Your body feels alive and perfectly healthy. You can breathe, and see, touch and feel. You are capable of walking, running, hiking or biking on a beautiful day of sunshine or rain.

You have amazing relationships with your family, spouse, children, pets, and friends. These relationships bring joy to your heart just thinking about them.

Your mind is alert and capable of reason and choice. You are free to direct ALL of your thoughts and feelings and you deliberately and with ease focus your thoughts on the beautiful, the amazing, and all the good in every person, place, and thing that you are in connection with in your life.

And you are overcome by the amount of goodness you see in your world, to the point that it brings you to tears of joy as you think about how wonderful life is and how blessed you are.

And then you get out of bed! This is just the beginning of your amazing day. You go outside and walk or run or bike and you are filled with joy as your body moves across the earth and you see the beauty all around and the deep love in the creation of this planet and your perfect body. You hear the birds, the sounds of people moving, and smell the earth, and it is so satisfying to your senses and to your soul.

Returning home, as you interact with the people in your life, your face is beaming with a broad smile as you see them and feel a deep sense of love for them.

You kiss them lovingly. You hug them, and hold them close for a moment feeling such a loving bond. Then you laugh as you discuss with delight the plans for the day and the week and the wonderful opportunities and unknown adventures that lie in store.

You thoroughly enjoy a pleasing, natural, light and delicious meal and you savor each bite. Life is amazing. You feel so happy and content. Yet at the same time excited and eager to go out, to move forward, and start giving and interacting.

You spend some time thinking, and writing in the quiet peace of your room or office or back patio, looking up to the mountains, or over the ocean, or simply at a beautiful picture on your wall. Your mind is clear and free from distraction or worry. Nothing can touch you or reach you in your quiet solitude. You are alone, and free. And you feel happy and excited to have thirty to sixty minutes to create and to explore the infinite depths of your mind and the infinite intelligence source that you are connected to and an integral part of. You write yourself the question that excites you or calls to you most in that moment. On white paper, with blue, easy flowing ink. And as you direct your thoughts on what you want to know or create, new thought trickles in, and you write and feel good. Then more comes, soon the trickle becomes a stream, and some days that is all. And it is good. You have more clarity and you have created more and expanded your life and mind. Some days the stream turns into a river of intelligence flowing into your mind. And you write and capture it as best you can. And it feels amazing.

Then you look in the mirror by your desk, and you see beauty, love, grace, mercy, kindness, goodness, passion, and compassion. And you see strength, and confidence, and power. And you are humbled by it. And supremely grateful. And you feel a deep commitment to yourself – to share the love you feel. To reach out and bless your fellow man. You feel the urge and desire to smile and warm somebody's heart that may really be missing and longing for love and compassion. You feel a deep longing to connect, serve, and bless as many as you can. And at least one other person. At least the next person you see. And you feel the desire to bless every person you see.

And you do it, starting with your thoughts. You leave your room or office and begin reaching out. Or you pick up the phone and begin your journey of blessing and serving. You see the beauty in them, and express it in your thoughts. You send them loving thoughts of gratitude, encouragement and compassion.

Every person in your perception receives a loving thought from you. And the world is better because you deliberately thought love. And your smile and the light in your eyes lift and bless everything in its wake. Then you act out of compassion and kindness, in all you do throughout the day. You don't even feel tension, worry, disappointment or fear. Those feelings are foreign to you, and the people, circumstances, and events that are attracted to you seem to be at peace. Your outflow of love and the frequency of gratitude and compassion at which you are living, attracts new and amazing people and circumstances into your life. Throughout the day you are in awe at life's beauty. At the grace and ease with which life flows and the universe provides everything for you in perfect timing and synchronicity. You see goodness and blessing in every circumstance and in every person. Even those that you would have thought were not helping you. Your mind is so filled with love, and so connected to your source, that you know without doubt that all things are happening for your benefit in some way, somehow.

At the end of a highly productive, growth filled, joyous day, you smile, and hug and kiss your family. You feel immense gratitude for your life and your relationships. You tell them how much joy they bring you, and how grateful you are to be with them.

If your children are at home, you kneel by their bed and have a wonderful moment talking about the beauty of this day, and the wonder of tomorrow. You savor each moment with each child, each loving word, and thought. You savor the peace. You are amazed at life and how blessed you feel.

As you lay your head on your pillow, your mind is again flooded with thoughts of gratitude for the abundance in your life. And your heart is filled with joy. You are satisfied with the day and the love that freely flowed through you throughout the entire day. And you feel excitement and enthusiasm for the blessing of a comfortable night of sleep that will lead to another wonderful day of life.

This is a truly amazing life.
This is my life. I live to love. And I love all of life.

Can you imagine living a life like that every day? Can you feel how just your attitude toward each moment of each day is really the only thing that makes it amazing or lackluster? It is all up to you.

That was my world at the time. A description of how many days felt. And reading back now, I feel so grateful that I wrote that down, because we all need reminders sometimes about the way to live. I must say that I struggled to live in that blissful state through many of the challenging, painful days to come. But I know from experience it is possible to attain.

But Could I Even Relate?

In summer 2012, as I began writing and creating products to help people stop having 'bad days', I felt that people would need to know that I could relate to hard times. So I searched my mind for the hard times I had been through in the past. But I can't say that I came up with a lot. Sure I had been through some hard times...but not nearly to the extent of some people I knew of. OK, I had a sore throat for a month. Big deal, right? Some people's trials make that look like a walk in the park. I wrote this in the early summer on my website.

TrulyAmazingLife.com
I Can Relate To Hard Times
"These days any time I see suffering, pain, and heartache, or discouragement, my desire to help somehow just gets stronger. I have experienced suffering and pain in my life. I have had plenty of 'bad days'. I couldn't even count them.

You might relate...like times not so long ago, when by the time I got home from work I felt so fried and frustrated, that I was totally useless to my family. I have been in the depths of sadness at times. I have felt depressed and discouraged. I have been ashamed of myself. I have felt weak and insecure. I have been consumed and overwhelmed at times by fear. I have been full of doubt and fear that I wouldn't stack up some days. That I wouldn't be able to provide for my family. That I wouldn't be able to pay the rent or mortgage. That I wouldn't be capable of doing the job. I have felt embarrassed and humiliated at times. I have suffered from envy and jealousy. I have been so stressed and anxious about my responsibilities that I got stomach ulcers after the birth of my first child. I have gone to food for comfort and felt shame and awkwardness because if it. I have neglected my body and been more than 30 pounds overweight; uncomfortable, unhappy and disappointed in myself. I watched as my mother died and felt the deep sadness of being separated from her when I was 18 years old.

I have experienced emotional suffering. I understand intimately how it feels. And so it is not without personal experience of suffering that I tell you that I believe this life is Truly Amazing.

I have seen how to stop emotional suffering and rise above it, and I want nothing more than to share that with those seeking it.

I realize that is a bold claim, but emotional suffering is just the negative emotion caused by a meaning we attach to things with our thoughts. And that is definitely within each of our control.

For example, I have experienced a lot of pain in the past that was completely free from any emotional suffering, because I saw the pain as good for me, rather than bad for me. And I know without doubt that it is good for me in some way. So not only can we avoid suffering mentally from pain, but with diligent thought, we can move to a place of acceptance and even gratitude for the good it is providing us."

I guess I couldn't relate to hard times well enough yet!! Those beliefs were about to be severely tested.

I had seen nothing yet.

A Tiny Spark Can Trigger Massive Change

July 28, 2012 was an extremely stressing day. Any time you add a new member to your family, huge changes are inevitable. But the birth of our daughter Kelsie lit the spark on a fuse that would soon reach a patiently waiting bundle of dynamite. Nan's description of the birth from her blog does the day more justice than I could:

In a postpartum visit with my midwife, as she was looking at her notes I asked her how long I actually pushed for because WOW that was the longest segment of time in my life. It felt like at least an hour of intense body wrenching and mind numbing pain. But no, not even close. "Twenty-one minutes," she said. Just twenty-one minutes.

At no point in my mental preparation or in the prenatal visits did we foresee a surprise breech detour but I do believe that God sends us on detours in life maybe so we can experience something new or empowering, or learn something profound. Maybe just so that we can learn to adapt. Most certainly so that we can grow.

Twenty-one minutes. Twenty-one minutes is probably about how long it took me to run my first 5K back in high school. Ready, set, GO! La-di-da...up this hill, down that one...oh there's the finish line, I think I'll sprint now...and it's over. I'm a little tired but oh, that was fun. **These** *twenty-one minutes, the final twenty-one minutes before I met my fourth child was much, much different. Exciting, yes. But not super fun and definitely not easy.*

I was pretty tired from being up all night, but birthing doesn't provide much opportunity for rest. Birthing provides opportunity for work. And let me tell you, that final twenty-one minutes was **work.**

After being told my baby was in the frank breech position and wondering **HOW IN THE WORLD AM I GOING TO PUSH THE HEAD OUT LAST!?** *There were some minutes in there where I found myself "hitting the wall" in absolute desperation, sobbing and screaming "I need to go to the hospital! Let's go to the hospital! They'll get this baby out* **now!** *" At which point one midwife shoved a spoonful of honey in my mouth and the other midwife calmly explained, "Nan, you are fully dilated and this baby is* **COMING.** *Trust me, it is much safer to deliver a breech baby right here at home than it would be in the car on the way to the hospital." She was right. At that point it was illogical to attempt getting in the car and driving to the hospital; time didn't allow us the option. Besides, my midwife knew what to do. She had caught no less than seven surprise breech babies before mine and everything was fine. As those thoughts went through my mind and the energy from the honey infused into my muscles and brain, my logic returned, I got my "second wind," stopped complaining, put my head down, and got to work. I visualized myself lying on the bed with a healthy, alert baby on my chest. I knew I'd be in that spot soon.*

For the record, pushing out a breech baby was much different than pushing out a vertex baby. It felt like two steps forward, one step back with each push. Or like I was in the final mile of a marathon where the race official announced, "Attention Nan Kennard, **YOU** *get to run an extra loop today! Please turn here. This will be your route to the finish line."*

While that slippery little bum ever so slightly inched its way out I knew the finish line was near, just not exactly HOW near or what kind of finishing kick I would have to lay down in order to reach it. Thankfully I had Aaron and two awesome midwifes patiently urging me onward. I could not have done that without them. In fact, I think my support team was even more than just Aaron and the midwives. There were moments when I felt strength beyond myself. Strength from God.

When Kelsie's legs popped out it felt like a catapult sling-shot right below me. The midwives quickly helped me turn from my position on my hands and knees to an upright position sitting on the birthing stool. As her body came out, Kelsie's arms had stretched up around her head so my midwife had to reach in and pull the arms and shoulders out one at a time. In case you're wondering, yes, that hurts. Once the arms were out, one midwife began fisting me in the abdomen with all her might to put pressure on the top of Kelsie's head while the other midwife gently pulled on Kelsie's chin to pull her head down into a more favorable position. They both told me to push like I'd never pushed before and what felt like minutes but must have only been seconds later, Kelsie was there! It was just 90 seconds between when her bum came to when her head came. The goal with breech birth is to get the head out no more than 5 minutes after the first part of the body. If it goes beyond that 5 minute window and the head has still not been birthed, the baby may have trauma. Kelsie only took 90 seconds, thank goodness!

*They put her on my chest and I rubbed her body to stimulate her to breathe. Even though she had not opened her eyes or taken her first breath I could feel that she was there. Life was in her. Her heart was beating and she was still getting oxygen from the umbilical cord, but still no breath. Moments later the midwives had her on the floor pumping air into her lungs while Aaron and I pleaded with God and Kelsie to **please breathe!** It couldn't have been more than twenty seconds but felt like an eternity before she took that first good* *breath and let out a heart-warming wail. That first cry was the most welcome baby cry I had ever heard. She let out a few more little whimpers and opened her eyes big and bright, then she was placed back on my chest and we just stared at each other for a good five minutes so happy to finally meet each other.*

*Ahhhhh.....it was finally over. That was the most I had ever yearned for a finish line in my entire life. And what a perfect finish line it was. An 8lb 9 oz, 21 inches long, **15 inch head** amazing little baby girl. Apparently a 15 inch head circumference is off the charts, above 100th percentile, whatever that means. Miracle is what it means to me. We witnessed a miracle to see the biggest part of her body come out last, just 90 seconds after of the rest of her body. Because, it could have turned out a lot differently.*

Now five weeks later, I look at Kelsie with amazement. Her entrance into this world was quite an exciting adventure and I'm sure she'll continue her life as such. We have what feels like a BIG family now with four awesome kids. Yes, it's busy and crazy and hectic at times but also fun and loving and abundant. I wouldn't want it any other way. Life is truly amazing.

My wife's strength and faith absolutely amaze and inspire me and I would be nothing today without her. To put her words into perspective, just a year earlier she literally limp-ran her way to a 6th place American finish of the 2011 Boston marathon in 2 hours and 38 minutes. Her quad cramped and seized less than half way into the race, and she grimaced in agonizing pain while still maintaining 6 minute miles for over 14 miles before collapsing at the finish line. And this after three previous natural childbirths. So for her to say this was "*the most she had ever yearned for a finish line in her entire life*" should give you some idea of the absolute intensity of the day.

27

And what may not have been clear from her description was how "life or death" the situation felt to us. We had both been awake for over 30 hours, since she started labor the night before right as we were going to bed. We were both exhausted, but especially Nan. And the situation of delivering a baby at home breach wracked our nerves. While it isn't as dangerous as the doctors at hospitals would have you believe, we had plenty of doubts and fears. As Nan started losing her mind in the hour before the birth, I struggled to hold it together and attempt to put on a strong and courageous face for her amidst intense stress and bombarding fearful thoughts. We bawled together, we prayed, and I tried my best to comfort her with words of assurance. I had to lean completely on the expertise and assurances of our midwives and somehow try to persuade Nan to do the same.

Then after navigating the 12 hours of an intense labor process came the absolutely crazy intensity of the birth itself. After what felt like 15 minutes (really only 90 seconds) of Nan screaming uncontrollably at the top of her lungs while pushing Kelsie out, to then find out she was not breathing was devastating! The thought that she may not live twisted our hearts into knots. Tears of anguish spilled out and all we could do in that moment was hold each other sobbing and praying to God to let her breathe...PLEASE LET HER BREATHE!

And of course she did breathe. And she was perfect and well in every way. The intensity of tears, and fears, and doubts and fatigue, were followed almost immediately by an incredibly powerful euphoria, joy, and happiness. This amazing little person had just successfully navigated her way to earth and to our family bringing total elation to our hearts, a magnificent contrast of feelings.

Here is a picture of our new family later that evening:

This picture accurately displays the state of absolute joy our entire family experienced that day. Those were not fake camera 'cheese' smiles. Words cannot describe well our feelings of elated fulfillment, despite it being ranked among the most challenging days for both Nan and myself. We felt deeply grateful to God. And our children absolutely adored their new sister and overflowed with giddy, happy laughs and smiles all day.

But little did any of us know at the time the unforeseeable challenge that extremely stressful day would trigger in our family. Nor the steepness of the descent from the magnificent climactic peak of pure happiness we all stood on. We thought we were prepared to welcome our fourth child into our home. But nothing could have fully prepared us for what came next. We couldn't see it, but a spark had been lit, and was now steadily devouring a fuse with explosion imminent.

Chapter 2

Let's Give A Warm Welcome To Our Good Friend Pain

Meet Your New Bunkmates

The day after Kelsie's birth, I noticed a minor burning sensation inside my butt. Weird. I didn't think much of it. The next day the burning worsened a little. The discomfort made sitting at my desk difficult. By the following day I could not sit down at all without major butt discomfort. Pain had wedged its toe in the door.

Four days later on a Friday, I finished my work by noon, using a newly jerry-rigged "standing office desk", made by stacking filing boxes on my desk to set my monitor and keyboard on. I could no longer sit comfortably for more than a few minutes. I had planned a camping trip in the mountains with the kids and some friends, so Nan could recover with Kelsie at home in peace. But when it came time to leave, a raging fire in my butt consumed me. Instead of packing the van, I curled up in the fetal position on my bed. Pain had now shoved its way inside the door and set up shop. And he brought his buddy Concern along for the party. OK, I admit my welcome doormat may have belied my true feelings in the moment as I attempted to close the door on them.

"What is going on here? Can we go back a week please and start this over? I'm pretty sure I learned my lesson with pain already. I'm good, thanks!"

"No? Bummer. Clearly I have more to learn…because this hurts!"

The intensity of Kelsie's birth day had clearly triggered something wacky in my body…but what?

It reminded me all too familiarly of waking up with nausea from stomach ulcers for three months starting the day after our son's birth eight years earlier.

Thankfully, after about 30 minutes lying down, the pain eased up a bit so I quickly packed the van, loaded the kids, and made the two hour drive to camp, shifting constantly in my seat. The pain finally died down that evening and happily we all enjoyed the evening roasting marshmallows and hotdogs.

The following week the pain intensified a little each day. In the mornings I felt OK, each afternoon severe burning incapacitated me, and by dinner the pain would settle down again. At 8 AM on August 9th I squirmed and shifted in the dentist's chair for 90 minutes. Root canal? No problem! The torture was the burning backside. Surviving that, I worked all day in moderate pain, mostly flat on my back in bed with my laptop. Recovered sufficiently, that evening the kids and I ran the "Pearl Street Mile" road race, a fun family event held each summer in downtown Boulder. We had trained for months. The kids did the half mile and then I raced the mile loop. Despite lying down in pain and discomfort most of the day, I had apparently recovered enough to run my fastest mile time ever – 4 minutes and 37 seconds. The goal of 4:30 was a stretch, so considering the circumstances, I smiled big at beating my previous best by 7 seconds.

However, the next day my new taskmaster 'Concern' had me scheduling with two different butt specialists (i.e. Gastroenterologists). But with the soonest appointment still a week away I had to somehow make peace with my new companions.

There Is No Bad Day

Meanwhile, my coffers still apparently overflowing with patience and positivity, I wrote this on August 13th on my blog:

TrulyAmazingLife.com

There's No Such Thing As A Bad Day

Will today be a good day or a bad day?

And why?

For me, today, and every day, is a good day.

Here's why...

Last year I realized that there is no such thing as a bad day unless I decide there is. I realized we all actually have the power to make today either good or bad simply by deciding.

I didn't fully realize that before then. I used to think that I wasn't in full control of whether I had a good or bad day. I thought bad days were an inevitable part of life.

I was wrong.

I no longer believe that, and I have proven it for myself. And I can help you prove it for yourself.

And it can make a massive difference in your life if you let it.

As I write this I am just barely recovered enough to type as the pain in my body has settled down a bit after about 4 hours of intense, burning waves of pain.

I'm not sure yet what is causing the pain in my body. I have two appointments with specialists scheduled.

Today I have been curled up in the fetal position for most of the last 4 hours, trying to breathe, be at peace, and learn from the experience. This has been a daily occurrence for the past week or so. I have been asking myself over and over, "Where is the benefit in this adversity? What is the advantage of this pain?"

I have also been reminding myself that "all these things will give me experience and will be for my good". And I know they will without a shred of doubt. I know absolutely, without doubt, that this pain I have been experiencing the past 16 days since the birth of my 4th child is here for a purpose. And I know that a lot of good will come from it.

I don't know how. And I don't know what yet. But I do know that it is for my good, and the collective good of all. And I consider myself blessed and feel very grateful for that faith.

*In the meantime, I am actively seeking knowledge and wisdom, clarity and peace within. **And I am finding them in abundance.** In November and December 2011, I experienced an intense sore throat pain that lasted for a month, during which I discovered how to enable that pain to become my servant, reminding me to **express gratitude and experience joy, even in pain.***

That experience embedded into my heart and mind the knowledge that my circumstances don't determine my life... my thoughts and my faith do. And right now today I am grateful for another opportunity to grow. I am grateful to have this new experience with pain because I know it is going to be for my good and enable me to do more good for others.

I certainly wouldn't have consciously sought out this experience. And it came seemingly randomly the very day that my daughter Kelsie was born on July 28. But I know that nothing is random. All things have purpose. And I will find the good in everything that shows up in my life. Because I know from experience that is the way to Joy and Abundance.

And I can tell you that I have not had a 'bad day' since December 2011. No amount of physical pain is capable of causing me to determine that today is bad. And if every day, the rest of my life, brings with it physical pain, then so be it. I know now more than ever that physical pain cannot and will not stop me from experiencing Joy.

Because I absolutely love today and I embrace it and I thank God for giving me another day of life. I thank our loving Creator for an amazing and beautiful, precious new baby girl. I am in absolute awe and amazement that I have the privilege to be such an integral part of this person's life.

I could go on for hours on how amazing life is and how blessed I am. As I write this, tears are streaming down my cheeks. Not from pain, but thinking about how full my heart is with the love I am surrounded by. My beautiful wife is sleeping soundly next to me, resting while Kelsie sleeps between meals. My 4 year old Ali and 8 year old Abe just came in to tell me with excitement of the 'Squeenky castle' they found on Amazon that Ali wants to buy with the money she earned weeding outside this morning. It is so wonderful to see the love Abe has for Ali, and the joy they experience together.

And I get to be a part of all of it! And I have the privilege of being called 'Daddy' and all the kisses and hugs and love that come with that. And I cannot hold back the tears. As I ponder and write about this it feels like my heart is overflowing out my eyes and trying to burst out everywhere.

I feel so blessed. I am so amazingly blessed.

So if this pain is here for nothing else than to remind me, and to remind you, to count our blessings, say thank you, and express our love, then it is sufficient. I will count it a worthwhile cost.

But I know there is more than that still. Our universal source and creator is eager to pour out blessings, abundance, goodness, joy, and happiness into our lives. Our task is simply to allow the flow. We just need to align our thoughts with the love and gratitude vibration that allows all goodness to flow to us and through us.

If we choose to think "Why me, why is this so hard? Why don't things work out for me?" Then we are choosing to stop the flow of goodness, abundance, love and peace into our life and we are holding ourselves apart from a truly amazing life.

Those thoughts are like paddling upstream. Just stop fighting the current and let yourself flow.

*Instead, **in times of comfort as well as pain, say "Thank You".** Look for the good in it. And keep on saying that. We will absolutely find reasons to be grateful. Say "I love you, God. I trust you, God. I love you, self. I trust you, self. You are capable and all knowing. I know that all things that happen are for my good, and I trust in time I will see how."*

And we will find the good in ALL things.

We get exactly what we look for. That is one thing that is meant by "Ask and ye shall receive."

So, will you join me in DECIDING that there is No Such Thing as a Bad Day? I invite you to do so.

This Is A Truly Amazing Life!

===============

Note: See the latest blog entries and join the Truly Amazing Life Community for free at TrulyAmazingLife.com.

Reading that now fills me with gratitude for the preparatory experiences of the previous eight months. Although, the commitment to never consider a day 'bad' could have been asking for it! I mean, seriously, what was I thinking to state publicly to the universe (or even all 5 of the people who read my blog) that *"No amount of physical pain is capable of causing me to determine that today is bad"?* God must have chuckled to Himself and thought "are you sure about that? Let's find out whether you really mean that."

OK, maybe, maybe not. But I'll tell you why I said it: I believed the truth that ALL things are for my ultimate good. And making the conscious decision to trust in that regardless of whatever comes our way is vital to experiencing a fullness of joy. If we wait until the storm overpowers us to decide how we will react to it, we are likely to make a poor choice. I think I was ready for even greater growth.

Life is painful. It's 'full of pain'. And there's nothing we can do to change that. Nor should we want to. **The question is what are we going to do about it?** We try and try to get around pain, to mask pain, to avoid pain at all costs, and numb the pain. But it's not going anywhere! It's part of the deal-e-o yo! So why not just embrace it and choose to see it for the good that it is even before it happens? Why not commit in advance to never considering a day as 'bad' ever again? That is called faith. And faith is literally power.

If you come up with a better solution than that, please let me know…I'm all ears!

Your Friendly Neighborhood GI Doc

A couple days later, at my first appointment on August 15th, the doctor seemed entirely unenthusiastic about his life in general. And he certainly didn't seem too pleased with his job choice of probing people's backsides for 40+ hours a week. To try to lighten him up I asked "so…how did you get into this particular medical specialty?" "It was a parole condition," he replied without even a hint of a smile or shift in his despondent expression.

Well, at least he was attempting to have fun with his job I guess? Clearly the thrill of exploring people's intestinal problems had long since passed for this doc and not an ounce of passion for his work remained. Either that or his wife had left him that morning. I confirmed it must have been the former when I learned later that a friend of mine had also recently been to the same doc and experienced the same attitude.

So my confidence in his diagnosis waned when he told me I just had hemorrhoids. He gave me some cream, and told me to call in a couple weeks if it wasn't getting better.

"Ummm…yeah, I'll be calling someone else. Thanks though!" (My thoughts, not words of course.)

The following week on August 22nd I saw a different GI doc who, upon examining my nether regions, immediately declared that I had an anal fissure as well as hemorrhoids. He gave me a new cream and some suppositories and sent me on my merry way with the standard "Call me in a couple weeks if it isn't improving."

Great, that should do it! He was very confident that this special cream would help me heal. Much happier with life and seemingly much more confident, I took heart in this new doctor's diagnosis and went back home to diligently apply my new cream every morning and night.

Well, another week went by and things got worse, not better. Now three weeks had passed and my new buddy 'Pain-tastic' started to really cramp my style. Each afternoon had turned into a pain management clinic between my bathroom and my bed. Annoying would be one fitting description.

August 30th we had one final evening race planned with the kids. But the night before, the burning in my backside intensified during the night and kept me hopping from bed to a hot bath tub for relief and back all night. You're probably thinking, "Ahhhh, a nice warm bath…I bet that was nice. What a lucky guy to get so much warm bath time!" Well, I'll have you know, that at 3 AM cramming yourself into a standard five foot tub is not exactly a pleasurable experience for a six foot two inch tall dude.

After maybe 2 hours of fitful sleep, I spent the day of the race recovering, still confined to the tub and my bed trying to sleep, or get some work done. No personal records would be set today. I barely had the energy to even attend the race to watch the kids run, let alone run myself.

There Is Something Good In This

The next day I wrote this email to my subscribers:

Subject: There Is Something Really, Really Good In This.

"What are the advantages to me in this?"

"What wonderful benefits are going to come out of this adversity?"

Those are the questions on my mind as I sit here in the tub this fine afternoon. And they are on my mind a lot lately. And they are sincere questions, and I fully expect and know I will find answers to them, or else I will create answers to them.

As it turns out, the tub is about the only place at the moment where I can induce relief from the burning pain in my back side. I set a shelf across the tub to hold my computer...a perfect portable water desk!

I will spare you all of the gory details, don't worry, but in brief I've been experiencing consistent waves of burning hot pain in the nether region for the past 30 days. I've seen 2 specialists and they are telling me it's an 'anal fissure' and it will just take time and some medication and fiber to heal. It is extremely uncomfortable. I got about 3 hours of sleep last night because of it, which has been an off and on occurrence the past month.

Meanwhile, I am content to let it heal, and I am intrigued and lifted as I search my mind for the answers to those 2 questions.

I share this with you for one reason, to give you the context for this question:

"What thoughts do you think to yourself when your circumstances become difficult or painful?"

Do you ever think any of these?

- *Why me? Why now?*
- *Of all the times this could happen, why now?*
- *I'm a good person, why do these hard things keep happening to me?*
- *Why does this always happen just when things are going so well?*
- *What did I do to deserve this?*
- *If there was a God, he wouldn't allow this kind of pain or suffering!*
- *I can't do this! I don't think I can go on another day with this pain. I think I would rather die than continue with this pain.*

Do you notice a trend in these? Life is unfair. I can't do it. Wah, wah, wah!

How are those types of thoughts helping or serving you?

How about these thoughts?

- *Wow! That hurts. There must be something really good in this!*
- *Ouch! I'm not a huge fan of that feeling. Hmmm...there must be something really good coming.*
- *What advantages will this pain bring?*
- *How can this benefit me?*
- *I don't like this feeling, but I know that this too shall pass. And I'm intrigued to see what good comes from this!*

- *This will be for my good, and give me experience.*
- *All things are working together for my good.*
- *What can I do to take advantage of this situation? How can I make this pain serve me?*
- *I know that every adversity carries the seed of an equivalent advantage. And this adversity is pretty intense. So there must be some amazing things that will come out of this. I'm going to look for them, and find them.*
- *I know I can endure this. And I know that it is making me stronger and better.*
- *I'm grateful that I have this opportunity to grow, and I intend to take full advantage of it and learn everything I can from it.*
- ***Thank you, God, for this truly amazing life experience!***

Do you feel the difference in the second round of thoughts? Do you think those thoughts might be more beneficial to you than the first set?

I know that they are. So my choice is to keep thinking the second thoughts.

And it is a lot easier for me to do that now than it used to be. Because thoughts are very habit forming. And I have been telling myself those thoughts for years and years now, so it's super easy for me to keep doing it now.

And because of all the amazing results I have experienced from thinking them, I have zero doubt now in their truthfulness. I know without doubt that all things that come into my life are there to serve and benefit me.

Do you know that? Beyond any doubt?

If you doubt that at all, I encourage you to just try on those 2nd set of thoughts for size. Just try them out next time you feel pain or hardship and see how they feel. Test them out and see what results you get. I think you'll be pleasantly surprised.

Then the doubt will be gone, because you will be exercising faith. And you can't be doubting and faithful in the same moment. It's one or the other.

And if you keep trying them, in time you will be in the habit of thinking the 2nd way, and you won't even bother with the first type of thoughts. They won't even cross your mind anymore.

And your life can then be nothing short of Truly Amazing. Then you will walk by faith all the time.

All Things Work Together For Your Good

When you get to the place where you have zero doubt that "all things work together for your good", life can be nothing but amazing. Because then there is awe, wonder, and amazement in ALL things.

Can you see that?

Can you see that the meaning you attach to everything is your own choice?

I want to help you choose to see all things as benefiting you. Because when you choose to see life that way, your life becomes Truly Amazing.

Please let me know how I can help you. I want to know what your concerns and challenges are with this. What is holding you back from seeing life that way?

Or if you just agree wholeheartedly and your life has been Truly Amazing for years, I want to hear your thoughts, too!

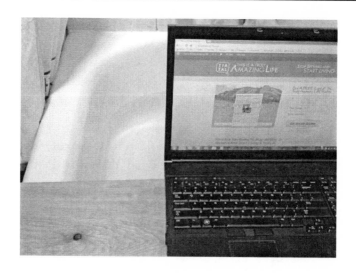

My Tub...My Temporary Solace

So from my tub, and in spite of the pain that is doing nothing to stop me from seeing my life as amazing, I invite you to choose to believe and see that ALL things that come your way are there to benefit you.

*And while I don't think I've yet found all the ways my current adversity will benefit me, I'm excited to find out! I do know this, **there is absolutely something really, really good in this.***

Remember...To Choose To See Your Life As Truly Amazing Is To Make It So.

-Aaron

===========

Note: A couple times in that email I mentioned thought habits. Since writing this I've actually created a system that will guide you to create the thought habits that will quickly eliminate negativity and fill you with positive thoughts and good feelings. Get access now at 5MinuteMentalMastery.com.

No, Seriously…Butt Pain Is Good!

The pain increased throughout the next week, and when I called the GI doc to report in, all he could tell me was to double the dose of cream.

"OK, but are you sure there's not something else going on? This is getting worse…it isn't getting better." I said. "These types of abrasions are really tough to heal because of where they are," he said. "You're just going to have to be patient with the process."

So I went forth doubling the dose of the cream. But seriously?? What was going on? Over a month of intensifying pain without a single sign of improvement? And what caused it in the first place? Nobody had any good answers for me. So I continued trusting the doctor and diligently applied my cream. He is the subject matter expert after all. And plus, look how official he looks in that white coat? Certainly he knows what he is talking about, he's a GI specialist! It will turn around…it just takes time he says.

Some days during the first week of September I curled up in pain nearly all day, constantly shifting from the bed to the tub for relief. Other days I felt fine and biked all day across town with the family. We rode to the bike park, enjoyed frozen yogurt on the way home, and I felt relatively normal. Well, except for the frantic searches for bathrooms every couple hours all across town…I guess there was that. But I was sure glad to have the energy to play with my family occasionally. And certainly this would pass soon enough; the doctor knows what he's doing. I'll be fine.

A wonderful habit I picked up early in the year is to write down as many positive things as possible about a topic on my mind; a super effective way to improve how you feel quickly. It's likely I felt oppressed by the pain when I wrote this in my journal that week.

9/4/2012 – Positive aspects of the butt pain – sitting in the tub

- *I'm becoming more capable of empathy and true love.*
- *It is enabling me to draw closer Christ in ways not possible without the contrast of this pain.*
- *It is teaching me what I am capable of.*
- *It is increasing my capabilities. I am now more capable of relating to people who suffer pain.*
- *It is reminding me daily to express gratitude for all things.*
- *The Spirit of God is strong in my heart. I can feel His love, compassion, and support. I can feel of His desire for me to experience a fullness of joy. This is one of my refining and character defining moments in eternity.*
- *It is an amazing opportunity for me to strengthen my FAITH and thereby increase my power to be an instrument in God's hands for blessing His children.*
- *What an honor and privilege it is to be counted worthy and capable of experiencing this much pain.*
- *God must have amazing joy in store for me which excites me immensely.*
- *There must be so much suffering of mind in the world right now that God needs me to help alleviate.*
- *I will do His bidding and His will.*
- *I willingly submit myself to whatever the Lord my God seeth fit to inflict upon me. I know His will is my everlasting joy.*
- *This pain is literally making me more like God. Thank you, God!*
- *This pain is showing me a deeper level of my Faith and bringing me closer to God.*
- *It's giving me lots of bath time! ;)*

- *It's providing a fantastic contrasting life experience which greatly enhances my joy- experiencing potential.*
- *It's providing me with a compelling story to tell. A story of pain, suffering, trial, conquering, Spirit over body, Faith and its literal effects, and unconditional love for God.*
- *I have the privilege of personally living and sharing a story that can relieve suffering and bring peace, harmony & joy to other's souls.*

It's kind of strange to me now reading that and remembering feeling the need to live this painful story in order help others in need later on. I don't know exactly how this story will bring 'peace, harmony & joy' to others, but something inside compels me to tell it. And I trust it will bless you who read it, and bring you greater joy somehow.

It helped me to focus my attention on the positive side of things. Every time I did, I felt peace and received strength. It wasn't easy though. It took concentrated effort to start the process, but it was always worth it.

Accepting Defeat

Despite increasing pain, I still ran my usual loop most mornings; an enjoyable and automatic habit I guess. It's hard for me to want to miss a day of running other than Sunday, because it feels so fantastic. Running is pure joy for me. I simply love everything about it. Some days I run slowly if that's what my body needs. I love just gliding up and down trails, or around the paths around town, soaking in the sun. For me, running is like plugging myself in and recharging my body and soul. Other days when I'm rested and recovered I like to do a challenging workout as part of my run, so I'll do series of hill sprints, or repeats around the track by my house. Those days are invigorating in a different way.

Regardless, running feels fantastic to me, which made it hard to let go.

But it became awkward and difficult suddenly with increasingly unpredictable bowel movements. On September 11 I found myself running as fast, yet as gingerly as possible back toward my house as my body threatened to give me a huge mess if I didn't get home quick. Phew! I made it just in time.

I could no longer run after that day. My situation took a nosedive directly into full debilitation.

Up until this point I had been teaching an early morning seminary class also since mid-August when school started. I was thoroughly enjoying the opportunity to teach the youth each morning about truthful principles that would guide them to greater happiness in their life.

And I felt a love growing each day for the kids, and a desire to see them grow in their ability to approach life with joy and achieve happiness despite all circumstances.

It took an hour or two of studying and preparing each night. But despite the sacrifice of time, and adjusting my morning work and running schedule, I thoroughly loved the opportunity.

But a severe challenge arose now that I found myself not sleeping much at all during the night. Some nights an intense burning pain in my butt would literally curl me up in a ball of agony on the floor. I wouldn't last long there, so I transferred to a hot tub full of water, which generally eased the pain substantially. But within minutes of leaving the tub, the intense burning would resume.

I found myself shifting and adjusting positions in my cramped tub in the basement for hours at a time in the middle of the night. And this now happened on a regular basis.

Not fun. But adding to the challenge, I knew I had to be dressed in my shirt and tie, and at the church ready to teach my young students at 6:30 in the morning. So by 4:30 in the morning,

I could no longer fall asleep for fear of not waking up and leaving everyone hanging out to dry with no teacher.

Somehow I pulled off the balancing act for a while. I would get out of the tub after a looooong night of discomfort and no sleep, throw on a shirt and tie, and head to the church to teach. I had some of the most touching experiences on those days as I would teach those kids and help them discover principles of truth they could apply in their lives. The connection to them felt deeply fulfilling. And many touching moments occurred when I knew they got it, and appreciated the lessons they were learning directly from the Spirit as the scriptures and truths opened their eyes.

But just standing up became increasingly difficult.

After one particularly difficult and painful night, by six in the morning I could barely get to my feet. I knew I wouldn't be able to stand up to teach. Or even sit down to make the 90 second commute to the church a half mile away.

I sent an email and text cancelling class.

I realized then that I was stressed. And my commitment to be there each day teaching added to the stress that I didn't really notice until now. But I sincerely wanted to be there with those kids. I didn't want to miss that class for anything. It totally bummed me out as I lay there in bed in pain. I think I must have gained as much, if not more, than the kids out of those early morning classes.

I thought I would cancel class just that day, but I never did make it back after that. From then on about 95% of each day I lay flat on my back or crunched in the tub. No more fighting it. Clearly running, teaching, and my businesses needed a vacation for a while. Time to accept a new reality: I'm sick. You win, body. I give. Clearly I need to stop resisting and focus on finding a solution.

Chapter 3

Digesting Digestive Disorder

Accelerating Decline

I found myself on a major detour from my planned route in life. Forget running, teaching, and my work, I couldn't even help with the dishes anymore. I couldn't help tuck the kids in at night. I barely had the energy to walk down the stairs, let alone run or play with my kids. The intensity of my concern rose daily as I lay there flat on my back in pain with increasingly bloody bowel movements.

"Why is this not getting any better? Why does this supposed specialist not seem to have a clue what is really going on with me? There has to be something else wrong!" We had no answers. My lifestyle had been completely shut down, powered off, and turned upside down and inside out. In less than a month I had gone from being a super energetic, take all three little kids camping by myself, conquer the world dad and husband, to feeling like a lump of worthless mass lying in bed, sucking the energy out of everything around me because I couldn't do anything for myself, let alone anyone else.

And suddenly concern for my wife's sanity skipped the line right to the front of my attention. Not only did she have a six week old baby girl who demanded most of her attention and energy, but now she didn't have any help with the huge needs of the other three young children. And as if that weren't enough, I couldn't even get my own food anymore! I could see her emotional reserves draining.

Early in the year I felt driven to automate and outsource my real estate business in order to spend more time working on what I felt my heart pulling me toward: helping others live a truly amazing life. I felt blessed to discover ways to automate and delegate that previously appeared impossible.

So now with my body shutting down, not having any stress about income was a major blessing! It's amazing to me how everything falls into perfect place in life as I follow my heart, and this was no exception.

I suppose I could choose to see things as not working out at all at this point since my body was technically killing itself. But I didn't view it that way. While I often don't understand trials in the moment, I know they will all be good for me somehow. I felt gratitude for the inspiration and motivation to unwittingly prepare for this illness financially. It brought immense relief during a time full of fears and uncertainties.

Clearly the way we decide to view things is largely our own choice. We can teach ourselves to look at things differently. If we constantly seek to be grateful our life will be full of miracles and blessings, even during the most difficult seasons.

I felt this was all for a good purpose, but I had no idea where it would lead. Nor could I see the purpose entirely. And as the whirlpool sucked us in faster each day, my situation quickly became a burden the entire family had to bear.

Unwanted Rituals

One morning after an especially intense night of little sleep, lot's of crying, and increased emotional despairing, I called my GI doc again and explained how much worse I felt and how my body's weight and energy steadily declined. I couldn't stand up much at all anymore, and now even hot baths were no help. Realizing the severity of the issue he scheduled me for the soonest available scope to see clearly what was going on inside me. In preparation they told me to fast for 12 hours and then do two enemas to clean my system within an hour before the appointment.

"Great, let's find out what's going on!" I thought.

By now I had read a bunch online and started hypothesizing that perhaps I had either Crohn's disease or ulcerative colitis. I sincerely hoped I had neither! Because the lifelong consequences of those chronic, incurable (according to the medical society) diseases looked daunting and undesirable to say the very least. But it could be even worse, like cancer. Now six weeks in and progressively deteriorating, I was desperate to know the cause and solution to this life-destroying pain.

The night before the appointment as I attempted to sleep the intense and burning pain resumed in its full non-glory. I retired to my bed of blankets in the guest bedroom at the back corner of our basement where I could perform my nightly bathtub rituals without constantly waking up Nan.

Lonely and discouraged in the middle of the night I tried to read, refilling the tub with warm water every hour or so. But tonight the pain didn't allow reading. So I focused on breathing. I tried to sleep in the tub. I tried to sleep on the floor in every position possible. But the burning waves would intensify and jar me awake. As I glanced at the clock, hoping beyond hope that I had slept for an hour, my heart would plummet seeing only eight minutes had passed. All night long I repeated this torturous game. And every glance at those red digital clock numbers stung worse than the glance before. But all I could do was shift from my blanket on the floor to the tub and back, all night. Constantly praying, begging for it to somehow miraculously just be seven o' clock already so I could take the enemas and get to the bottom of this insanity.

When 7:00 AM mercifully arrived, I prepared one of the salt water fleece enemas that seemed to have no problem patiently waiting all night, mocking me from their comfortable place on the night stand. I inserted it, squeezed in the fluid, and lay on my side to wait as long as I could before rushing to the bathroom.

After just a couple minutes I rushed to the toilet for the impending flush of my system. The moment I squatted over the toilet the most painful burning I can ever recall ensued. Trumping all previous burnings! How does this keep getting worse?? An involuntary scream of agony roared out of my mouth. I think every muscle in my body contracted as I screamed in agony over that toilet.

Unprepared for that kind of pain, it taxed and overwhelmed my entire system. But it passed and I wobbled back to my bed on the floor to catch my breath and recover.

"How am I going to survive another one of those??!?" The thought made me cringe and curl up in a ball and I cried. "I don't know if I have it in me to go through that again." I whimpered to myself and to God.

But I had to do it. I couldn't risk not being prepared for the camera and risk delaying my diagnosis even further. So after about 25 minutes of resting and talking myself up, I braced myself and inserted the second enema. "Here goes!" I lay there and waited for the ensuing explosion of pain. Less than a minute later I dragged myself to my feet and speed-hobbled to the bathroom.

"AAAAAAAHHHHHHHH!!!" Equally if not more intense this time. I screamed, and moaned, and cried in pain until everything was out. The process zapped all my energy, and sent me into a dazed state of bewilderment and sadness.

"How can this be the state of my life? How can I go on dealing with these insane levels of pain? This is just getting worse and worse!" Tears flowed freely.

What You Give, You Receive.

No sleep the entire night capped off with the full body workout intensity of those two enemas had me lying on the floor feeling barely alive.

I knew I needed to get myself up the stairs and get dressed so I could make it to the doctor's office for the procedure. But I couldn't muster the energy to do it initially. It took a good 30 minutes before I finally recovered enough to work my way upstairs, stopping multiple times in the process.

On the way out the door with Nan supporting my instability, we found a small package of envelopes on the doorstep. As I fully reclined myself in the passenger seat of our van I opened the package and silent tears streamed down my cheeks. My seminary students had written me cards that morning and left them on my doorstep.

It could not have been timed better. I felt as low and discouraged as I could ever recall feeling. Their gesture touched my heart and filled me with gratitude and love. Soon it was another full on sob-fest on the way to the hospital as I considered the unknown darkness and pain coming, and felt of the love and compassion of these young friends.

Here's a small sampling of the letters:

Dear Brother Kennard,
Get well soon!! We miss you so much in class! You've been gone for too long. Hope you get feeling much better really, really soon!
♡
P.S. Have you memorized all of the actions? I haven't yet... but I will!!!

"Dear Brother Kennard, Get well soon!! We miss you <u>so</u> much in class! You've been gone for too long. Hope you get feeling much better really, really soon! P.S. Have you memorized all of the actions? I haven't yet...but I will!!!"

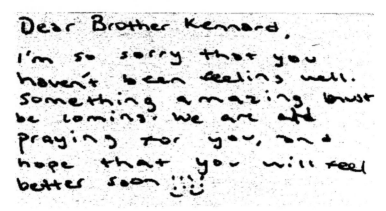

*"Dear Brother Kennard, I'm so sorry that you haven't been feeling well. **Something amazing must be coming**. We are all praying for you, and hope that you will feel better soon ☺ ☺"*

This one touched me most of all that morning:

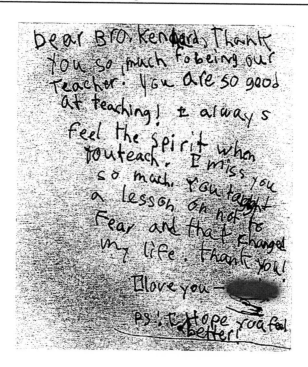

"Dear Bro. Kennard, Thank you so much for being our teacher! You are so good at teaching! I always feel the Spirit when you teach. I miss you so much. You taught a lesson on not to Fear and that changed my life. Thank you! I love you – XXXX – P.S. I hope you feel better!"

I found it so beautiful that one of these amazing youth would repeat back to me one of the principles I had recently shared in class: that this adversity meant that something amazing was coming. I knew she spoke the truth. And it filled me with strength and hope and willpower to continue forth and be a little stronger in that discouraging time. And as I remembered teaching them how fear is the opposite of faith, I could feel God filling me with faith. I lay there in awe as the love I felt melted fear away.

As I write this tears of joy flow again. What is that feeling? Why is it so indescribable? I can't say that I know for sure, but I do know this: I love that feeling. I relish every occasion when I can feel this level of emotional connectedness to myself, to my source, to the spirit of love and life that flows through me. I absolutely love this feeling of being alive in this moment...of feeling a joy, a peace, and a happiness that is so intangible, but yet somehow I'm touching it and feeling it flow through me. These moments are real living. When I am not distracted by guilt, or remorse of the past, or fear of inadequacy in the future. When I am simply thankful, hopeful, joyful. When I appreciate the beauty that is surrounding me right now.

In that moment in the van on the way to the doctor's office I knew that everything was fine. The Spirit of my Creator warmed my heart, comforting me, telling me not in words, but with an indescribable yet undeniably clear and perfect knowledge in my soul that all is well. That this too shall pass. That I would be OK. In fact, better than OK. That amazing things were coming. Things I had no way of even understanding at that point.

Like a ray of light piercing through dark clouds of fatigue, discouragement, sadness, and fear of the unknown. And that ray lit a small fire in my heart, just big enough to give me a taste of joy amidst the pain, and strength to move forward.

Chronic And Incurable

Soon we arrived at the hospital and I hobbled into the lobby and up the elevator. I leaned over the counter to check myself in with the remaining energy I had, and then sprawled on the floor in the waiting area. They helped me onto the hospital bed and administered mild sedatives, putting me out of my misery. "Thank you!" I only vaguely recall the procedure starting and looking up at a screen and hearing the word ulcers. Then I fell asleep.

When I woke up the doc informed me he saw ulcers which indicated ulcerative colitis (UC). But a tissue sample sent for a biopsy would confirm the findings. They wheeled me out in a wheelchair and we went home to wait two days for the findings to come back from the lab.

On Friday morning, September 22, unable to restrain myself I called the doctor at 9:30 in the morning. Nothing yet. Waiting all day I filled the time with research on UC and Crohn's, and hoped it was only UC.

UC, according to the doctor, is localized just in the large intestine rather than being spread through the entire digestive tract. So they said it should be less invasive to the body and easier to manage.

Finally at about 4 PM the doctor called me and confirmed the results did indeed show UC. At least they were 99% sure of that.

A slight relief, since I had braced myself for the worst. But it's still a chronic, incurable condition according to the doctors. Nice to now know what is happening...kind of. But is there really no cure? "This will never go away completely. " He told me. "You will deal with this disease the rest of your life."

Say No To Drugs! Except...

"So what's the treatment?" I asked. "What do we do now?"

"We start you on a pretty high dose of steroid, called Prednisone," the doctor said. "Go fill the prescription I'll send to the pharmacy right now and call me in about 10 days to report in on the progress."

I picked it up immediately and took my first pill, filled with a weird sense of contentment and relief because it felt so good to finally think I knew what was happening. The doctor seemed very confident, so we placed our hope and trust in him and went forth with the drug.

Within five hours of taking the pill, I noticed improvement in my output. "It's working already!" I told Nan excitedly. I slept easier and felt less discouraged than I had the entire month so far.

I had just received a diagnosis of a chronic disease that had no known cure and would plague me the rest of my life. The doctor told me I would take medication for it until the day I die. Yet, strangely, that was comforting and made me feel much, much better than not knowing what was going on. I guess it's not that strange though…I guess it makes sense now that I could see a pathway out of the pain. "Great, give me the drugs! Whatever it takes to get rid of this insanity of pain, I'll do anything at this point!"

Physically I felt better already the next day. I still didn't have enough energy to get out of bed, but I did feel better.

Reflections On A Chronic Diagnosis

As Nan brought me a lunch in the bed we had set up in the back living room, I gazed out the window at the perfect, sunny, autumn afternoon. I watched my beautiful wife and children getting ready to head out and my heart filled with gratitude. I wanted to go out and play with them, and I might have been a bit bummed that I was bedridden. But I felt contented gratitude. As they left, I grabbed my journal off its make-shift brown leather couch ottoman nightstand and wrote:

> *9/22/2012 – 3:00 pm*
> *Reflections on a Chronic Diagnosis*
> *My beautiful wife and children just excitedly left to go swimming. I am remaining here to rest and to watch over Kelsie.*

My body has been relatively pain free today as long as I'm lying down. I am so thankful for the reprieve and rest from the physical pain. Yesterday I received a diagnosis that my body currently has the condition known as "ulcerative colitis" which means that my colon has ulcers in it due to my immune system attacking my healthy cells from what I know so far.

Why is it doing this? I don't know. The cause is not determined in the medical community apparently and therefore the permanent solution has not been found either according to the doctors. Supposedly I have a chronic disease or disorder.

It's an interesting position to be encountering myself in. On one hand I am ecstatic to feel like I have a proper diagnosis because now I have been given a drug that has already in the first 5 hours stopped my bleeding.

On the other hand, it naturally seems unfortunate to be given a chronic disorder to be able to deal with for the rest of my life. But then as I consider it, I immediately must say and am inclined to believe that it is not unfortunate at all. In fact, I firmly believe that it is actually most fortunate.

I cannot with perfect clarity and knowledge explain all the ways in which it is a very good thing. But I believe it is. If it were not for my best and the good of the universe in general, it would not have taken place. I believe that to accept that unforeseeable and unavoidable conditions are detrimental, is to deny the existence of goodness in general. If God's aim is our glory, growth, and all good things, then to me, to espouse the belief that some things we are allowed to pass through are for our benefit, and others are there with the purpose of harming us, would be putting God in contradiction with Himself. I frankly think it's a ridiculous notion and I don't buy it.

Instead, I hold and will continue to maintain even stronger now having experienced such recent suffering and diagnosis – that Everything is conspiring for my benefit.

I simply know that it is. It cannot be any other way. Otherwise the very meaning of all things would be thrown into question.

So where am I now? Where do I now stand in light of recent intense sufferings of pain endured and a "chronic" diagnosis obtained?

Do I now go forth in life in fear and trepidation as I wonder when the next round of debilitating pain may take over? Certainly not.

So how do I reconcile this? How do I reconcile myself to the will of God?

I must confess thoughts of defeat and despair have not entirely avoided me over the last few weeks of agony as I lay 95% of the day on my back on the floor, and suffer intensely painful bowel movements constantly full of blood for weeks at a time. Is it not natural to experience those despairing thoughts? Absolutely!

Really, how could I not have some despairing thoughts and still be considered alive and reasoning? Because I had such amazing, comfortable, joyous, and pain-free circumstances just 8 weeks prior. Of course the feelings of grief over the loss of those comfortable circumstances were natural at that point! And I definitely felt that grief. There is such immense contrast and such a huge difference between my daily activities currently and what they were two months ago.

And I cannot say I enjoy the latter more, far from it. In fact I desire more strongly than ever those comfortable days when I was completely unencumbered by my body's limitations.

So what do I do now? How shall I respond to the moment I now face? In despaired longing for what I had in the past? NO!

How about discontented wishing for the future circumstances to come sooner? Absolutely not!

How I shall respond is with gratitude and awe at the beauty and wonder of it all.

How amazing is it that I am actually capable of suffering such intense and relentless pain with no apparent cause? I don't know how, but somehow I survived it and it passed for the moment. And I know if it happens that I have future pain, I will be fully capable somehow of getting through that also. What's more, I am intrigued and fascinated by the search for meaning in it all. Because quite frankly, it excites me a lot as I think of the amazing potential for good that is being created by way of this painful suffering. I know there is something amazing coming as part of this, and it is fun to wonder about it and look for it.

Who can I now help with my increased depth of ability for compassion and empathy? There must be thousands, maybe millions suffering pain right now who can use compassionate understanding and uplifting words and energy. Am I not now more equipped to lend a hand? Am I not now a sharper, more effective instrument in the surgeon's healing hand? Yes! Yes, I am.

I know more than ever what it is like to suffer unavoidably. And I know it is possible to find goodness and meaning in it all.

And so I respond with gratitude, awe, and wonder. I'm grateful to be alive and coherent, and feeling gratitude in this moment. I'm grateful for all the trials and adversities as well as the prosperity and abundance I am blessed with. Because who am I to claim to know whether something, someone, or some event is bad for me? In fact, better said, who am I to assert in defiance of God, that anything he allows me to go through is for my detriment? That would be pure absurdity!!

I absolutely believe God when He has repeatedly said that all things work together for our good. Certainly if I choose to oppose goodness through my own hatred and selfishness and purposefully fight against goodness then I'm causing my own misery. But to suggest that our creator, the source of all that is, the source of life, light, and everything else, all knowing, perfectly loving, and all powerful, could or would intend harm upon us?

That is absurd. There is nothing about that thought that makes any sense to me.

So I will stick to what I know works and what will serve me immensely: **the belief that everything is conspiring for my benefit.**

I love that belief! It is so inspiring, hope giving, and good feeling.

I love to search for and find the beautiful and good in all things. And I view the past 2 months of intense pain and suffering as a holy and sacred time in my life. I am honored and humbled by the experience. Honored because I feel God's immense love for me, and I see more than ever how strong He knows I am. I feel Him preparing me, refining me, and sharpening me for His service. And humbled by the same token. I know that I am being refined for a great purpose and I'm humbled and grateful to be viewed worthy and capable of great suffering and thus great leadership.

To conclude for now, I don't know what this evening will bring, or tomorrow, or next week. I don't know whether I'll be in massive pain or whether I will feel perfectly whole. I do know this. I will keep doing everything in my power to feel whole physically. And I will hold high in my mind continuously my ideals, which are to serve and bless my family, and to serve and bless humanity. I will spend my free moments elaborately envisioning and creating my ideals in the canvas and workshop of my mind. I will focus my attention on clarifying the details of my visions and ideals. And I will do everything in my power to serve those around me and to heal my body so that I am in a better position to serve and bless others.

I am so indebted and grateful to my amazing and strong wife Nan. She is an angel to me, as are my children, all serving me selflessly in my time of adversity.

Thank you, God! This is a truly amazing life you have given us.

What a beautiful day! What a welcome, soul-recharging reprieve from the emotional and physical pain.

What I knew that day was I felt grateful, humble, and optimistic about the future.

What I didn't know (which probably good because it would have squashed those amazing feelings flat on their face) was that was only round one. I had no way of seeing that round two would soon begin, and that it would be twice as challenging.

Chapter 4

Round 2: High Hopes

"I'm sure you've discovered my deep and abiding interest in pain. Presently I'm writing the definitive work on the subject." – Count Rugen, The Princess Bride

The SCD – A Miracle Cure?

On September 25th I read most of the book "Breaking the Vicious Cycle" by Elaine Gottschall in which she outlines a complete recommended diet for Crohn's disease and UC called the "Specific Carbohydrate Diet" (SCD). Incredibly motivated, I implemented the diet the next day. Apparently hundreds of people had used the SCD to either cure or allow them to live with Crohn's or UC without drugs and without pain. I followed the diet religiously. Like a zealot even, much to the vexation of Nan who had to deal with the repercussions of a now extremely picky eater with extreme dietary requests. As if she didn't have enough on her plate already.

Two days later Nan wrote this email to our families, updating them and informing most of them for the first time about our situation:

From: Nan Kennard
Sent: Thursday, September 27, 2012 4:52 PM
To: Family Group Email
Subject: Call for Prayer

Dear Family,

Will you please consider fasting and/or praying with/for our family? Aaron is in a great deal of digestive/colon pain that began the day after Kelsie was born. At first the Dr. thought it was just an anal fissure from the stress of the birth and new child but his symptoms have become much worse and debilitating over the past few weeks. He has lost 10+ lbs and is now bedridden and very weak. After a colonoscopy last Wednesday the doctor suggested that it may be ulcerative colitis.

He has begun pharmaceutical and nutritional treatment, which helped stop the bleeding but he is still feeling very sick. We are hopeful that his condition will improve over time as we figure out what foods he can eat that will provide nourishment without running right through him. We will also probably get him in for a blood test soon to see if he is anemic and treat that.

In addition to Aaron's illness, Abe is mentally un-well and is crying all the time, hating school, and clearly stressed out. His stress is likely related to Aaron's illness, the new baby, new school routine, etc.

I am doing my best to take care of a newborn, an invalid, and three other needy kids and it's overwhelming. I know all these things are for our good and will make us better people in the long run but right now it feels heavy.

Our Ward has been very supportive and helpful with bringing meals and setting up play dates for the kids. It's interesting that even in the midst of feeling the refiner's fire blast against us, I've shed tears of joy when I think of all the blessings we DO have.

I have a testimony of the power of collective prayer and I know God is mindful of us. Thanks in advance for your love and concern. I love you all and hope you all are doing well and feeling happy.

Love,
Nan

After receiving responses of grave concern and worry from many of our family members, I wrote this in response:

From: Aaron Kennard
Sent: Friday, September 28, 2012 10:31 AM
To: Family Group Email
Subject: RE: Call for Prayer

Thanks everyone for the thoughts and prayers. Sometimes when it rains it pours, which can definitely make life interesting! (If painful.)

Here are a few of my thoughts really quickly:

Please don't worry about me! All is well. And all is good. All things give us experience and are for our good. There is absolutely nothing that has happened or can happen to remove us from God's love and His watchful care and guidance. He knows exactly why we are being allowed to experience this super challenging circumstance and He is always with us. And while I don't claim to know all the ways, I do know with absolute certainty that amazing things will come out of this. God is all-knowing, all-powerful, and all-loving. Everything about this is perfect and is happening for a very, very good reason.

Silver metal that is being refined certainly is not eager to be burned in a fiery pot to remove it's imperfections, but it's willing to do so, trusting in its creator and knowing it is necessary for its ultimate purpose, joy, beauty, and betterment.

So just know that not only am I going to be totally fine, we are all going to be much better off because of this. I'm figuring out what to eat and how to treat it and my body will get back to normal.

So thank you for your thoughts of faith, compassion, encouragement and love. We feel that, and are blessed by it. Your positive energy and love is amazing.

And for those who may feel fear or are worried for any reason, please try not to spend any of your valuable energy worrying. Worry is based in fear that something bad may happen and is not productive since it is in opposition of faith. There is nothing bad that can possibly happen. So be of good cheer, and see God's hand and goodness in it. As I lie here, and despite bowel pain and diarrhea, I am in awe and amazement at the beauty of life and the goodness of God. And it certainly doesn't make much sense to me that others might be worried or despairing on my behalf while I'm feeling so much love and peace.

Thank you again for all of your care and desires to help! We really appreciate it. The biggest challenge for me is feeling incapable of helping Nan with the burden of a newborn and 3 other young children with a lot of needs. Nan is so strong and capable, but it's a big weight to bear. So thank you for your attempts to lighten the load. Nan's Mom is coming over to help in about a week which will be a huge blessing.

Life is amazing!

Love, Aaron

The next few days produced significantly motivating and encouraging improvement. The bloody bowel movements had stopped. I still had painful diarrhea all day long, but at least the blood had disappeared. And by Sunday I even had enough energy to make it to church for 90 minutes. Ahhhh! To be out of the house for a change!! My body is on the mend! This diet is working!

Days earlier I couldn't be out of bed much at all and on Monday I only lay for a total of an hour in bed during the day. I even took my son to the store that evening. I'm loving this! Thank you, doctors, and your prescription drugs. Thank you, Elaine Gottschall, for your amazing work and diet. Whatever is causing this improvement, thank you, God! I'll take it!

These days I wore man-diapers full time to mitigate the risk of blowouts all over the carpet or my bed. Since that would be far too nasty and annoying to deal with, I opted for the less messy, if not humiliating 'Depends'. And I would definitely not leave home without them!

In the middle of the night of October 1st I woke up like normal in an urgent rush to the bathroom. But this time I actually passed a piece of stool that could be discerned as a stool, not a runny mess! Hooray!! And it didn't even hurt that bad! Wonderful news to a stool connoisseur like me, who spent no less than two to three hours each day performing and analyzing bowel movements. Stools were my new specialty and this was amazing! The pills are working! The diet is working! Ha ha! I'm going to be OK! Yes!! Normal poo has returned!!!!!

So entirely stoked by this major fecal development, my mind raced and I couldn't fall back asleep. The possibilities reeling of getting my former pain-free lifestyle back. My two-month companion of burning tight butt pain had disappeared since starting the steroids. "This is good. This is a miracle," I thought.

There's A Pill For That

But as I lay there, not falling asleep, slowly the tight, burning in my butt returned.

"What?? No!!! I thought we were past this??"

Soon it was a full-fledged burnout and by early morning total discomfort again.

"What kind of cruel joke is this? Just as I was getting my hopes up they are dashed to pieces on the ground!" I thought in total disbelief of this immediate turn for the worse.

And just like that, improvement stopped dead in its tracks. I returned to the tub for comfort as a super painful morning ensued. The pain eased off later, but the entire night following I rushed to the bathroom every 2 hours as my entire system voided itself of all liquids. Thankfully it wasn't painful this time! But by 6 AM I was spent. With my last remaining ounce of energy I stood myself up from the toilet and felt like I would pass out. I managed to make it into my bedroom where Nan was stirring, and I crashed on the bed in total exhaustion. Extremely dehydrated after the all night liquid expulsion, my stomach now started cramping up. The pain had now moved from butt burning sessions, to stomach cramps and entire body fatigue.

I could barely talk and I definitely couldn't move anywhere. Even lying on the bed I thought I might pass out, which highly concerned us both. I tried to drink some herbal tea with honey to get some calories and fluid in. I managed to drink half of a water bottle in a couple hours. That gave me back some coherence and ability to speak. But still frightfully dehydrated, and now nauseous, and cramping, I tried some chicken soup, and couldn't force it in. By 9 AM I frantically begged Nan to take me to the hospital to get an IV of liquid into my system. Severe dehydration threatened to shut my body down soon.

At the ER, I hunched over the counter to check myself in. I could barely get my name out and I must have looked like death himself hobbling in there. Yet to the receptionist this must have been just business as usual. "Oh hey death, come on in. Just sign here and here and we'll be with you in a couple hours." She might as well have said with her nonchalant demeanor. She casually entered my information in no rush whatsoever. Eventually finishing her silent typing, and with no indication of sympathy or urgency, she motioned me down the hall.

"What kind of EMERGENCY room is this??" I thought. "I'm dying here!"

When she introduced me to a nurse I asked if they had somewhere I could lie down. Finally the nurse kicked people into overdrive and they wheeled in a hospital bed for me on the spot. Thank you!

I spent the next three hours in the ER getting filled up with two liters of IV liquid and pumped full of some kind of powerful pain killer. It knocked me out for a solid 90 minutes and WOW, what a relief! When I came back to the land of the living, Nan and the doctor and I discussed our options: more drugs. Oh wait, I guess I should have said 'option' singular. They had consulted with my GI doc and concurred that I should increase my dose of steroids, and start another drug mesalamine to combat the gut inflammation. That afternoon I walked out of the ER feeling half way decent thanks to the re-hydration, pain drugs, and a nice nap. But how frustrating to hear that the only solution was more drugs! I was beginning to see that when it comes to 'western medicine', there's a pill for everything, but nothing has a cure.

Someone has done an excellent job it seems...of changing much of the medical community's perspective from one of preventing disease through health and proper nutrition, to treating disease with synthetic drugs. There's something wrong with that picture. But in my state I could not question. I needed anything that could stop the destruction.

The Ultimate Weight Loss Program - Do NOT Try This At Home!

At 2 PM on October 3rd I weighed 161.4 pounds. By 9 PM I only weighed 158.4. Highly disconcerting. We're supposed to weigh more at night not less!

I kept hoping this latest attempt at a solution would work. This time the increased steroids and the new drug should definitely be the ticket! This had to work. In combination with the new diet, certainly I'm going to start pulling out of this!

And I did feel a bit better for a few days. But yet my weight kept dropping. By the morning of October 7, I was down to 156.2 pounds. And two days later I was down to 153.8 as recorded in my journal. I had begun meticulously tracking every single piece of food I put into my mouth , every single bowel movement in full detail, as well as how I was feeling. Intensely interested in discovering what helped and what hurt me, this had become my new major purpose in life. It demanded all of my attention and I was determined to fix this problem. There had to be something I could do! 16 pills per day and just waiting and hoping did not do it for me. So religiously I wrote everything down to analyze patterns, causes and effects.

But despite my efforts to eat everything I could (within the guidelines of a new diet), my weight kept falling fast. 25 pounds in a month! On September 1st I weighed 178 pounds. This was not a trend I could afford to continue. But what more can I do? I felt like I was improving a bit, so surely it will turn around soon.

But I could never find reliable patterns despite all my tracking attempts. Just when I thought I saw improvement I would start feeling horrible for no apparent cause. I was so meticulous about the food I would eat it was driving us all insane. For all the food Nan prepared I grilled her about its contents and sometimes discovered she had added an 'illegal food' unwittingly. "Sorry, I can't eat that." I felt horrible for the burden I loaded on my patient and loving wife. But I was testing a new very rigid diet that specified what I could and could not eat in no uncertain terms. So to deviate from it at all, in my mind, would nullify the results of the test.

Nan kept telling me that stressing too much about the food I ate could itself be exacerbating my problems. I sensed she was right, but I didn't know how to back off, I needed a solution! So daily I sent Nan off to the grocery store for some new food item from the 'legal' list to try out, which amplified a stressful situation.

You can imagine how much this drained Nan, especially when added to the constant needs of our now two month old daughter, and our other three kids. Already beyond maxing out her capabilities, the kids grew whinier and needier daily as they received little attention from either of us.

Life Saving Love

During this increasing turmoil, our extended family and friends responded graciously and amazingly. People started showing up with food almost every day, removing the burden off Nan's shoulders to prepare each meal for the kids. Then my parents drove in from eight hours away and stayed with us for days to help cook, and clean, and take care of the kids.

After they left, Nan's mother flew into town for over a week to help. She took time off from her teaching job and hired a substitute so she could help us. What a life saving blessing they offered us. We can't express how thankful we are for all the loving help in that crazy time.

Just to have them there to talk to, pray with, and commiserate with was an enormous help emotionally for both of us. But the physical help of going to the store, cleaning the house, doing laundry, and cooking food was equally rescuing. All the little things in life that are quite manageable with two healthy parents to divide and conquer, suddenly become an insurmountable and overwhelming challenge when one of those people is removed from the 'helper' side of the equation and placed on the 'needs help' side. Looking back I'm not sure we all would have survived, literally, without the compassionate, selfless service of our family and friends.

A New Hope

The blood in my stools had returned and along with it came new pains. So much for the steroids fixing everything! However, my undesired companion for two months, the burning waves of butt pain throughout the day and night, had gone away entirely! And it did not leave unnoticed, believe me. I was enormously grateful to bid it farewell! Unfortunately, in its place came bloating, extreme fatigue, accelerated weight loss, and moodiness.

Hmmmm…not sure I like how this bargain is weighted…but I'm glad the all night tub sessions are over!

Clearly neither the SCD nor the drugs were resolving my problems. There had to be something else I could do! I kept searching. On October 9th, I got "The Maker's Diet" by Jordan Rubin and read most of it that day and the next. It gave me new hope and new motivation (and it gave my wife the burden of a new shopping list to acquire ASAP). Essentially, Jordan tells his inspirational story of having had severe Crohn's disease and at 6 feet tall getting down to 104 pounds at one point and very near death. At which point he found a mentor who guided him in implementing a whole food based, healthy diet that helped him completely recover and heal from Crohn's disease.

I'm a believer, sign me up! I need those results, and I'm willing to try anything! Very similar to Elaine's recommendations with the SCD, I resonated with the logic in it. So I made a few tweaks to the SCD, not many, and implemented his recommended diet.

Hopeful and optimistic again, I believed this could be the ticket and that Jordan's recommendations in combination with the SCD would somehow help me recover and get off pharmaceutical drugs completely.

Once again I noticed slight improvement right away. For the next few days my weight stabilized, and I even found the energy to get out of the house a couple times. All physical exertion still highly taxed my system though and sleep would overtake me. But I still felt things were improving slightly, and I held onto that glimmer of hope tightly.

Nan wrote this to our family on October 13:

From: Nan Kennard
Sent: Saturday, October 13, 2012 9:41 AM
To: (Family Group Email)
Subject: Update on Aaron

Hi All,

Thanks for all your prayers and positive thoughts for Aaron. We have definitely felt your love and God's watchful care these past couple of weeks. We have had many tender mercies from the Lord and I know He is mindful of us.

Last week after a sleepless night of pain and dehydration, and after a few hours in the ER, some IV fluids, and blood tests the doctor there said she would admit him to the hospital if I was feeling too overwhelmed by it all. They could keep him on IV fluids and give him drugs that would let him sleep OR we could just go home and keep trying to hydrate and rest in bed. Aaron really did not want to be in the hospital alone on drugs and hospital food and I didn't want to leave him there, so we opted to be released and come home.

Mom and Dad Kennard came out the next day and stayed for the weekend. They helped with cooking, cleaning, entertaining kids, cleaning the yard, and fixing things around the house (thanks so much, Mom and Dad!) They also drove Ali back to Utah with them and she is staying with Emily and Ashley for a couple of weeks until Dawn drives her back on the 18th.

This week, Mom (Alyson) has been here helping with cooking, cleaning, organizing baby clothes, entertaining kids, and shopping as well. It has been SO nice to have the help and has really boosted moral in our home. I'm a little anxious about how I'm going to do it all when Mom leaves, but I keep thinking optimistically and am hopeful that Aaron will start improving and he will be able to get out of bed more and feel better.

The doctor put Aaron on a pretty heavy dose of immunosuppressant and steroid drugs right now in an effort to reduce inflammation and stop his immune system from attacking his intestinal wall. He has never been a big fan of prescription drugs but is following the doctor's suggestions while also trying to fix his diet and remove anything that may be fueling the fire. His diet consists of well-cooked veggies, chicken and beef stock, and a little meat. No grains, legumes, or sugars, and very little fruit. Before this flare up started a month ago, he was a healthy 178 lbs, running 60-90 minutes a day and feeling great. Now he is 153 lbs and his daily exercise consists of waddling to and from the bathroom. He was able to stand up a little bit more this week and last night we actually went on a "date night" to Whole Foods to get a new probiotic supplement and some foods to try. He made it to the vitamin aisle before he had to sit down and go back to the car. He is very weak and just cannot stand for very long.

We have been working closely with a nutritionist who cured her own Crohn's disease through diet and she is trying to help us get Aaron's diet dialed in. Over the next couple of weeks we also have appointments with a few more doctors to get some more blood work and second and third opinions. We want to be sure he has the correct diagnosis and also get some opinions about which drugs and diet are best for treating it.

Things to be grateful for this week: Aaron's weight seems to have stabilized (not much loss this week) and his appetite is improving. Visits from Grandma Suzi, Papa Duck, and Grandma Evans have lifted our spirits and been super helpful and comforting. Abe seems to be doing a little better with his attitude and communicating better about his feelings (he was SUPER stressed out and sad a few weeks ago). Breanne is a little angel and helps me SO much. Ali is having a blast with her aunts, uncles, and cousins in Utah (THANK YOU, Emily and Ashley!) Kelsie is growing well and is a happy, pleasant baby. And last, but not least, we have SO many loving family and friends who are pulling for Aaron and praying on our behalf. THANK YOU!!!

Love,
Nan

There was hope! Things had to start improving, right? We were doing everything possible.

A Shattered Hope

That same day, October 13th things took a turn for the worse again.

I now required pain pills to sleep at all; the bloating in my bowels now too intense all the time. And the next morning the scale display read 148.2. "NO!!! I thought things were stabilizing! That's the wrong direction. It's OK. Stay calm. Something's going to give. It's going to turn around, these things just take time. I need to allow time for the diet and drugs to do their thing."

I calmed myself down, and was able to enjoy much of that Sunday, being with my children, and even playing a board game with my son as I propped myself up on my side in my bed in the living room.

Then at 2:00 AM the next morning I woke suddenly to a major urge for a bowel movement, and barely a moment later before I could even move it all came bursting out. Here's my journal entry description: "Massive quantity of dark blood came out in bed and got everywhere. Huge fist sized blood clots came out also."

"What is going on!?!! This is freaking me out!" The blood loss, the blood clots, the increased pain and bloating. I didn't know who to talk to. My GI doc just kept saying the same thing – take more drugs – and I had lost all confidence in him. This was worse than ever, and I had been following his advice for nearly two months now! I need a new doctor! I felt a desperate need for another opinion. There had to be something else wrong, or something else we could do. The drugs weren't working. The diets weren't working.

The truth stood fully exposed, glaring me right in the eyes. I could no longer deny and convince myself I was healing.

I was dying.

Chapter 5

Desperation, Confusion, Insanity, Cookies

Emergency Room 2.0

Facing reality head on can be hard. But my body's self-destruction had to be faced. I was losing an average of one pound every single day. I knew I couldn't sustain that rate for long. Already feeble, it required all my mental and physical strength just to lift myself out of bed and onto my feet.

That morning Nan and I held each other and cried for quite a while after she got the kids off to school. At a loss, we called the only other place we could think of to get additional help, the University Hospital. My GI doc assured me they would say the same thing he was saying, but I saw no other option than to try. Their soonest opening was nearly three weeks out. The only way to jump the line was the emergency room. In desperation we packed up and made the 40 minute drive. I'm pretty sure fist-sized blood clots and severe weight loss daily constitutes an emergency.

Nan pushed me into the ER in a wheel chair and we joined over 40 other people waiting to get in. Since I didn't 'appear' to be imminently dying, we waited...and waited...and waited. We sat for hours in the ER lobby as I shifted constantly in discomfort in my chair. Once they finally gave me a room in the ER, we had the agonizing experience of a new ER doctor who knew nothing of my condition and who had no idea what to do with me. After he heard my story and took an X-ray of my bowels, he recommended I go home!

"WHY DO ALL THESE DOCTORS SAY THE SAME THING!?!", I thought. Furiously I flipped out at the doctor: "I'm not going anywhere! My wife cannot take care of me. She's not capable of handling my needs and giving me medical attention. We have four young kids at home who are freaked out by watching me dying, and my wife is freaked out watching me withering away. I am not going home until someone figures out how to help me! I can't continue to survive losing a pound every single day. If you send me home you're sending me off to die! What do you expect me to do? Are you telling me there's nothing you can do and I should just go home and die? Sorry, that's just not an acceptable answer to me."

I demanded to speak with the gastroenterology specialists, refusing to go anywhere until I saw the specialists for my disease. When the doctors were gone deliberating, Nan and I just cried, and prayed, and pleaded with God that somehow they would admit me, and get the specialists to treat me.

Over an hour later, a nurse finally came in and informed us they decided to admit me and give me a room. THANK YOU!!

I could almost see the weight lifted from Nan's shoulders as relief flowed into her face. She desperately needed a break from caring for me at home.

Trust Me!

Hospitals are wonderful. But you can get too much of a good thing.

What a huge relief to have nurses waiting on me at all times! Nan desperately needed a reprieve from that burden. I stayed in the ER cubicle overnight, and the next day got moved to a nice suite with a view of the mountains and my own bathroom! Living the high life now! It's the little things in life, right? They had me on constant IV hydration which restored my energy fairly quickly. And I also had IV steroids, as well as IV pain drugs, all of which significantly improved how I felt. But the hospital brought its own new challenges:

- Day and night prodding with needles
- The frustration of no good answers
- Arguments with doctors about diet
- Loneliness creeping deeper daily
- Agonizingly repetitive and undesirable food choices

I began updating my family and friends daily on Facebook and email from the hospital, here's how the week went down:

Facebook

October 16, 2012

WOW! Perspective changes everything. I'm starting prep for a CT scan in 1 hour and the nurses braced me for this nasty contrast fluid I need to get down. I was in HEAVEN sipping the whole thing down slowly! I slurped every bit out. It seriously tasted like an amazing new Slurpee flavor to me and brought me a huge grin and laughs with my CNA. After 24 hours of ice chips...barium sulfate is great it turns out! I can't wait to start the next bottle in 5 min. Life is good;). (We'll see if I'm still raving after 3 of these bottles.)

October 17, 2012

I get to keep my colon which I'm thankful for. No surgery urgent at the moment.

But I still don't have a solution to the piercing, consistent pain. Probably need to try a different drug approach, should get recommendations later.

40 hours on ice chips so far minus the little barium sulfate binge last night. Good times!

October 18, 2012

I was feeling good enough to sit up to eat today...pretty nice to be out of the bed for a change. And the view is a lot better from over here. They need to see how I'm progressing tomorrow and then we'll know how well the approach is working.

So all the doctors I have spoken to are ADAMANTLY telling me to trust them that it makes no difference what I eat. That I can eat anything on the menu and it will not possibly hinder my progress in any way. The drugs, they say, will remove the inflammation, and the food is inconsequential.

But I can't bring myself to believe it for some reason. Part of me wants to believe them because it would be so much easier. But how is it possible that what I put into my colon has no effect on it?

An Email to Nan:

From: Aaron Kennard
Sent: Thursday, October 18, 2012 10:16 PM
To: Nan Kennard
Subject: Re: Food log

I want to talk to more doctors. I want to know what is going on. I'm concerned because my internal hemorrhoids are bulging out more and more with each BM and they hurt. I'm getting pretty frustrated by doctors. Tonight I asked the nurse what it would take for me to be able to talk to one of the two specialists in IBD here. I want to speak to someone else, just to at least see how they respond to my questions. My current doc seems so confident in himself. And he looks me straight in the eye over and over and says 'trust me, it doesn't matter at all what you eat'.

What am I supposed to think about that? Do I just get over it and realize that's what all these doctors think? I feel like I need to at least talk to some more doctors. I feel like I need a doctor I can relate to and understand. If it doesn't matter what I eat, then why is all this pain when I have bowel movements happening now that I'm eating again? I can accept that perhaps regardless of what I eat right now I will have this pain with the movements. But then how am I supposed to heal while also eating when I have all this pain, diarrhea, and bulging insides?

I didn't take any pain meds during the day and I felt fine. Tonight I'm going to take as much I can in order to hopefully sleep.

I love you. I miss you. I hope you are OK.

I actually had a 30 minute argument with my GI doctor and four of his fellows and students one afternoon. I hardly believed he could look at me with a straight face and tell me that food had zero effect on my condition. How could anyone say that? Food has no effect on my digestive system? Really? You're joking, right?

Nope. They weren't joking. And it took a 30 minute argument for me to finally be worn down enough to just accept what he was saying.

"So you're saying I can eat anything I want…burgers, brownies, ice cream…anything! And it won't have any negative effect on my progress!?"

"Yes! Trust me. Just trust me!"

That's what he left me with. Trust me. And believe me… I really wanted to trust him. I was in a super vulnerable state. Clearly the diets I had tried didn't work. And the GI doctor used that to prove his point. I had a hard time arguing with that because I knew that none of the dietary changes made me any better.

So I trusted him…kind of. I could never fully trust him though, because what he was saying was too far removed from logic and common sense for me to fully believe it, even in my weakened and vulnerable state. But I did decide to take him up on it, and enjoy the food while I was there as best I could.

They Shall Mount Up With Wings As Eagles

I still ordered the gluten free options. I couldn't bring myself to go back to eating gluten yet after everything I had read decrying it as a gut inflammatory with huge negative consequences. So that week I ordered the gluten free burger and in my starved condition it was simply delicious. And I ordered the gluten free waffles, which were like tasteless cardboard. But smothered in butter and honey they were divine to me at the time! And I ordered the gluten free brownie for dessert! The only sugar I had eaten in the past few weeks was from honey and fruit. So the brownie was supremely satisfying to my sugar deprived brain that was so addicted to refined sugar and chocolate. After that I ordered dessert at every meal! And at breakfast I ordered the blueberry muffins with my eggs.

But my guts were just screaming at me. As I trusted the doctor and kept eating, my guts were constantly bloated, and my severely painful bowel movements like clockwork came every two hours. Only heavy doses of drugs were enabling me to make it through the days without total agony all the time. By the time Saturday morning rolled around, I felt I was going insane. My hospital bed felt like the sleeping bag of my youth that my brother would trap me inside of kicking and screaming. The repetitive life of lying in a hospital bed, being prodded and poked with needles all day and all night, and constantly moving from bed to toilet in severe pain, all took a huge toll on my mental and emotional state.

It was an extreme challenge to be happy some moments. But my weight was going up! And that was motivating. And I did feel a bit more strength every day. And finally by Saturday the doctors and my wife and I all agreed I could go home. Nan was hesitant and scared though, unsure how she would care for me at home on her own. I appeared to be on the recovery path...kind of. And I really did think I would go crazy if I stayed there another day. It didn't seem they were doing anything for me anymore.

That morning Nan came and rescued me and took me home.

I posted this the next day on Facebook:

October 21, 2012

I gained a few pounds in the hospital this week and I'm seeing slow forward progress. I think I am on the recovery path. Though from where I stand it looks like a pretty long path.

The hospital stay was a blessing. But after 6 days in 1 small room dragging my IV between the bed and the bathroom...I thought I might go insane.

Yesterday morning at the hospital was one of the lowest feeling times in life I can remember. I was becoming overcome with negativity and discouragement despite the progress during the week. All I was seeing was a pretty bleak life for some reason.

But my angel wife Nan came and rescued me. And thankfully I came home last night. Home sweet home has never meant more than yesterday. My 4 year old Ali couldn't stop hugging me and her beaming smile and love felt so amazing.

So now I will keep taking one shuffle step forward at a time, until I am back to taking normal steps...and then running free again. 2 months ago I ran a personal best of a 4:37 mile. I will be running again someday. For now I'll be taking a bunch of pills and pain meds and doing my best to find the good in and make the most of each moment I have.

Thank you all so much for your loving, positive thoughts, prayers, and energy toward me and my family. We feel it and are so grateful.

This promise lifts my soul and carries me in the darker moments:

Isaiah 40:28-41

"Hast thou not heard that the everlasting God, the Creator of the ends of the earth, fainteth not, neither is weary? There is no searching of his understanding.

He giveth power to the faint; and to them that have no might he increaseth strength.

Even the youths shall faint and be weary...

But they that wait upon the Lord shall renew their strength; they shall mount up with wings as eagles; they shall run, and not be weary; and they shall walk, and not faint."

Reading that passage now brings tears to my eyes. I can't help feeling overcome with gratitude at God's grace and mercy. I love that promise. I know it is real. I have witnessed it over and over in my life. Now I fainted almost daily every time I walked. And I certainly wasn't running anywhere anymore, let alone doing it without being weary. Yet running was such a fulfilling and positive part of my life. So trusting in this promise gave me hope. I believed deeply that it was true, and that I would run again, and walk and not faint.

Chicken And Clay

But I still had no clue how that was going to happen. Or what I needed to do. When I got home from the hospital, a new book had arrived in the mail called "Restoring Your Digestive Health" by Jordan Rubin and another doctor. It contained more specific recommendations tailored specifically to my diagnosed disease, and the only option I saw was to give it another shot. I still couldn't bring myself to believe the GI doctors and just eat anything and everything. My heart just wouldn't allow me to believe them yet.

So I started in earnest the next day doing a 14 day cleanse eating nothing but chicken soup, mineral water, and liquid clay (bentonite).

Every night I had my family shut the door to my 'suite': a soundproof living room addition at the back of our house where I was sleeping. That way nobody would hear me screaming and moaning all night long with every bowel movement. Very quickly I started noticing improvement in my output, though I still had no less pain or moaning or screaming.

On October 24th I was feeling enough energy to stand up for a bit, and I asked my friend Eric to take some pictures of my deterioration for posterity. I thought surely I couldn't get much skinnier than this and I hoped I was at my lowest point.

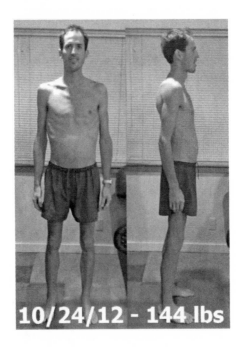

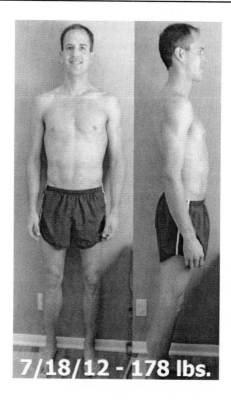

7/18/12 - 178 lbs.

I happened to have taken some pictures just three months prior as part of a before/after series of photos I had started in 2009 when I was 30 pounds overweight and needing some motivation. I had no idea when I took these 'after' pictures in July that they would become 'before' pictures in a new disease progression.

The next day I wrote this on Facebook:

October 25, 2012

It's hard to know how my body is doing right now.
Everything is so cyclical I often can't tell whether I'm getting better or worse. Yesterday I felt better all day than I have in a

91

long time. I was still in bed all day, but not in much pain and able to work on things and be productive. It felt good.

Then last night I was in extreme pain off and on throughout the night and no amount of Percocet seemed to be helping anything. It was really rough. I'm getting a slight reprieve from the pain this morning. But this is such a crazy, intense, persistent challenge. It's hard to describe. It's a big roller coaster... but not the fun kind.

But somehow I know it has to pass. I know I'll get beyond this and be better because of it. And meanwhile, I'm going to do my best each day to heal. And I'm going to do my best to make the best of my situation.

My firm belief is that this is a Truly Amazing Life. Even despite the current struggle I am in. And this belief has been put to the test for me nearly daily for the past 3 months. And it continues to pass every test.

I am in the thick of the battle right now with a disease that is trying to take me down. But I am determined more than ever to live to the fullest and continue my mission of helping others live fully.

Thanks again for all your prayers and support for me and my family in this intensely difficult time! I feel so blessed by it all.

My morning breakfast on Thursday October 25th: 5 partial spoonfuls of chicken soup and 2 tablespoons of clay.

Certainly the soup had been deliciously prepared by my angel wife, but my body didn't go for it. I felt like heaving just thinking about eating it. Still on the 8 to 10 pound per week pace of losing weight, I was literally starving to death. I knew this couldn't last.

So I force-fed the chicken soup for the 5th day in a row. But I couldn't get much down. Finally that night I cracked. It had been four days of nothing but chicken soup and liquid clay. This was the cleansing part of the latest diet I read about in Jordan Rubin's book, and I was supposed to be improving. But I wasn't. In fact the pain was worse than 4 days earlier.

I couldn't do it anymore. So I quit.

I asked Nan to just get me some 'normal' food. I can't remember what I ate that night, but I do remember it being supremely satisfying. That morning was the last time I kept track of my food, totally burned out after tracking it for nearly two months and finding zero improvement.

The next day I called my gastroenterologist and amazingly got in to see him that day at 2 PM. He scolded me for not eating and told me to start eating anything and everything I could. I was beyond tired of trying to figure out what to eat and starving myself anyway, so despite the fact that I still couldn't logically agree with him, I decided to take him up on it. I couldn't argue with his assessment that I was starving myself.

After the appointment Nan picked me up a huge, juicy burger. I lay down sideways on the bench in the front lobby of the doctor's office (my butt in way too much pain to sit up), loaded on a packet of High Fructose Corn Ketchup and mustard, and went to town. "Who cares how bad this hurts coming out! It couldn't be worse than the burning I already have. And even if is, I'm done starving myself!" Then I devoured the sweet potato fries with only one lament: I was out of fake tomato sugar to dump all over them.

"Mmmmmmmmmm! Food!! What an amazing concept!"

Peace Amidst The Rage

That evening Nan went out with the kids to a gathering with some friends and sent me this text of a statement someone made:

> "Sometimes the Lord calms the storm. Sometimes he let's the storm rage and calms the soul."
>
> Fri, Oct 26, 2012, 6:13 PM

"Sometimes the Lord calms the storm. Sometimes he lets the storm rage and calms the soul."

The storm was certainly raging for us at this time. But through it all, we were consistently blessed with peace and calm in our moments of greatest need. I can tell you from experience that statement is true. That reminder helped me that day. I did feel at peace that day, despite the fact that nothing improved with my pain (I do have to give some credit to the burger though;).

While she was out, some friends dropped by to visit and brought a heaping plate of heavenly brownies, cookies, and marshmallow caramel delightful treats. At home alone with no energy to stand up to get food, their timing couldn't have been better. I devoured three or four of the delicious baked goods, and thanked them profusely for coming by right at that moment. I asked Paul to kindly fetch me a heaping glass of milk, and oh how I enjoyed that combo after a week of starving on chicken soup.

As my friends left and I fell asleep I felt relatively good about life. Even though the pain storm raged on that night and I was up every two hours dealing with painful bowel movements, I somehow felt things would get better now. I fell into my two hour sleep shifts in relative peace.

Chapter 6

A Journey Through Hell

Explosions In The Night

At 3:15 AM on October 27 an intense burning in my male parts suddenly jarred me from my dreams. Immediately, shocked screams of agony filled the room.

"OW! OW!!! HELP! HELP!!!"

But nobody could hear me. My soundproof chamber of a living room with all the sliding doors closed fulfilled its duty perfectly. But tonight that posed a problem! Different than anything I had experienced prior, this sharp, stabbing pain came on fast and was not letting up. Unfamiliar pain is far scarier than the tried and true.

I screamed out "Help! HELP! NAN!" again in vain, realizing she couldn't hear me. Fortunately I always kept my phone right by my bed. I grabbed it and frantically dialed 911.

As the operator picked up I did my best to be calm and answer the questions, but it was tough to even breathe, let alone get coherent words out.

"I NEED AN AMBULANCE!" I panicked into the phone.

"What is your name?"

"Aaron Kennard"

"Can you tell me what's wrong?"

"OW! OW! PLEASE HELP!" I screamed into the phone. "I have ulcerative colitis and something is exploding inside me!"

"What's your address?" I blurted my address then more screams and moaning to please send help quickly.

"Can you get to your front door?" She asked.

"I DON'T KNOW! I'LL TRY. HELP! PLEASE HELP!" I shouted panicking.

"Try to make it to your front door and stay on the line, the ambulance is on its way."

"OK," I said, as I slumped off the bed and crawled toward the door.

I managed to pull the sliding door open from my knees amid moans of "OW! OW! HELP! HELP!!" All I could think to do was keep yelling and begging for help. Nan immediately woke up to my screams and rushed into the kitchen. Horror painted her face as she saw my skeletal naked frame screaming in agony crawling across the floor. Moments later a knock rapped on the door...it could have only been a few minutes from when I made the call.

"What happened? What's going on??" she demanded. The front door swung open as freezing winter mountain air rushed in with four EMT's.

"I DON'T KNOW! I DON'T KNOW!" I shouted in loud monotone.

"BLANKET! BLANKET!!" More shouting. "WATER! I NEED WATER! IT'S GONNA BLOW! IT'S GONNA BLOW UP!!! BLANKET!!"

"What's gonna blow?" she asked. "What's wrong??"

"I DON'T KNOW! MY GROIN! I DON'T KNOW!" Fiercely shivering now and still screaming, they loaded me onto a stretcher and asked for my name and birth date. Explosive pain threatened to burst me to pieces. They piled three blankets over me and I rolled out the door and into the waiting ambulance. More questions as they strapped me into place: "What's your name?" "Aaron Kennard!" I replied. "What's your date of birth?" they asked. "Didn't they already ask me that two times in the house?" I wondered. I told them again. "They must be testing to see if I'm coherent. Yes, I'm here! And I'm exploding!! Please help me!!" My mind raced.

One EMT sprayed a pain drug into my nose. No relief. Then the ambulance flew down the road with sirens blaring. "Please God, let me live! I don't want to die. Please help me!!" were my thoughts. From my mouth came "OW!! OW! AM I GOING TO DIE?"

Nothing like any pain I had ever experienced, I had the distinct feeling death was imminent. I didn't fear dying for my own sake. But thoughts of my wife and children's well-being consumed me and I deeply yearned to stay alive for their sake, the thought of leaving Nan alone with our four little kids simply unbearable. Overwhelmed, I could only keep asking, "AM I GOING TO DIE? PLEASE HELP ME!"

In the living room at home, broken and dejected on her knees, Nan sobbed uncontrollably. "Please, Heavenly Father! Please don't let him die! Please let him be OK!!! PLEASE!!"

Emergency Room Protocol

The explosive pain lasted about 90 excruciating minutes, finally easing off around 4:45 AM. Everyone at the ER seemed to be moving in slow motion. They had given me an IV of liquids and my pain had slightly eased, but nobody knew what to do with me, as usual. I told them of my diagnosis of UC, but they couldn't see a connection to that with the pain I described. It didn't make sense to me either, but clearly something was drastically wrong.

They wheeled me to a different room to do an ultrasound and x-ray. About 15 minutes later they informed me I should probably just go home because they couldn't see anything wrong.

"WHAT?!?! ARE YOU KIDDING ME?? NO!!! I'M NOT GOING ANYWHERE! There is something wrong with me and I'm not leaving until you find out what it is. What's with these ER doctors always trying to send me home!?!"

I couldn't believe they had the nerve to say I should just go home and wait it out. "Wait what out? Are you not hearing what I'm telling you? I'm in agony here! I'm in severe pain! I can't keep living with this kind of pain. I need you to figure out what is wrong!" How many times do I need to repeat this torturous ER doc convincing process?

About that time, a new wave of pain began, welcoming back my moaning and screaming, this time, focused in my bladder, which suddenly felt like exploding! The nurse came in and I frantically told her "I need a catheter! My bladder is going to burst!"

"We can't give you a catheter unless we know you really are full, we can't risk infection otherwise."

"IT'S FULL! IT'S GOING TO BURST APART! PLEASE, PLEASE JUST GIVE ME THE CATHETER! THEY HAD TO GIVE ME ONE LAST WEEK WHEN THE SAME THING HAPPENED. PLEASE! IT HURTS SO BAD!!" I cried and screamed frantically.

"Sorry, we have to do an ultrasound before we can give you a catheter."

"AAAAHHHHHHHH!!"

What seemed like 15 minutes later and was probably closer to 3 or 4, they came in with an ultrasound machine.

"Wow, you're full alright".

"HELLO!!! THAT'S WHAT I'VE BEEN TRYING TO TELL YOU! ARE YOU DEAF OR SOMETHING?" Is what I thought in my head…how infuriating to be writhing in pain and have people with straight, long faces, slowly going about their business following all the protocols to the letter. I could hardly believe it. In their defense it was 4:30 AM and they were just doing their best to help me within the regulations they had been given. But when you're in massive pain, it's really easy to get frustrated and impatient. I was not myself. Fortunately they brought in the catheter, drained my bladder, and soon the intense explosive pain subsided.

The 3rd Time Is NOT A Charm, Trust Me ;)

I had a reprieve for 30 minutes or so. Then they informed me they needed to do a CT scan in order to get a better look at what was going on inside.

I didn't think I could do it. I knew from the CT scan a week and a half earlier that I would have to drink about a half gallon of liquid and I was petrified it would burst me apart to even try.

They said it had to be done…so they gave me the fluid and I started choking it down.

After succeeding with one of the two bottles, I simply couldn't force myself to drink anymore. The nurse kindly allowed me to forego the second bottle and they wheeled me to the CT scan room. The bladder pain had not come back yet, so I had the CT scan in relative peace and returned to my room to await the results.

But by the time I got back to the room, a third wave of pain began. This time my guts felt like they were exploding. Soon I would find out that was literally true. But in the meantime, it felt like the exploding of my bladder, but now encompassing my entire abdominal area, and even worse than the bladder if that is even possible. I screamed for help again.

"Am I going to die??!" I panted panic-stricken to my nurse. "Is this what it feels like to die?"

They didn't know what to say. So I kept screaming. And I kept asking.

How is it possible that this just keeps getting more intense? Nan and I were convinced that something more than ulcerative colitis was wrong with me…this was different than everything we had been told and read about it.

Nan had to go home to coordinate a new babysitter for the kids, and soon I found myself alone, for a long while. It felt like an endless while, alone in my cubicle in the ER, waiting to learn my fate and hoping for some answer. There has to be some solution to this! I moaned, dejected, dangling from the last remaining strand of hope left in me.

Drum Roll Please

Finally the doctor and nurse came back with the findings from the CT scan.

"Your colon is perforated in several places. You need surgery as soon as possible."

"Please! Anything!" I thought. "Something! Thank you!" Finally we are getting somewhere. Finally they are acknowledging that something is actually wrong with me…as if it weren't obvious enough from my uncontrollable shrieks of pain all morning long! But at least we are finally getting on the same page and they aren't trying to send me home!!

"Yes! Please! Get me to the operating room. I don't know how much longer I can live with this pain."

I texted Nan with my limited energy:

> **I'm perforated. Need surgery todqy**
> Sat, Oct 27, 2012, 9:08 AM

But I had to keep waiting. It was now 9:08 in the morning. My throat was parched and they wouldn't allow me any liquid before surgery. My body ached, and my bowels throbbed, still feeling like they would burst apart any moment. Nan rushed back to the hospital to be with me.

They had given me drugs through the IV, and perhaps that was helping, but I couldn't be sure. I prayed and begged for them to get me to the operating room and put me under. Put me out of this misery!

Soon they wheeled me into the operating area where I met my surgeon. He explained that in all likelihood he would need to remove my entire colon, which I had no idea until recently, is the same thing as my large intestine. He further informed me I would then have an ostomy bag: a plastic bag to catch the output directly from where they would eject my small intestine through a hole they would create in my abdomen.

"Is that the only option?" I asked. The surgeon assured Nan and I he would do everything he could to save my colon but that it didn't look promising at all.

Then he left Nan and I alone to consider the situation. There was really no choice at this point. My body's deadly toxic situation needed to be stopped fast. We said a prayer to God together, imploring Him to guide the surgeon and bless his efforts that I would live and the operation would be successful. We cried and I could see the fear in Nan's eyes. Nothing I could do to comfort her, I just told her "It will work out. I need to have the surgery fast." I desperately needed to be put under and stop the painful agony. She told the surgeon to move ahead, and I learned later, mandated him in no uncertain terms to save my life.

I managed to scribble a mock-signature on all the consent forms, and they brought in the anesthesiologist. "Please, just put me under!" I thought, and said to them. "Please put me out of this misery." Soon they placed the gas mask and I felt myself slipping into relief. "Ahhhh…thank you! Thank you!"

Here's a Facebook post from Nan that afternoon while I was under the knife:

Nan Kennard - October 27, 2012

We have had a crazy day. Aaron woke up at 3:30 am in searing pain, called the ambulance and went to the ER screaming and wailing. I was left home with my four sleeping kids and began to pray and call friends relentlessly until someone finally picked up and rushed over to my house so I could go be with Aaron. One test led to another and now its 9 hours later and I am sitting in the surgery waiting room to hear how surgery went. They had to remove his entire colon because it was clogged and perforated. Definitely one of the most stressful and scary days of my life. I hope it gets better from here. Awaiting good news from the surgeon...

Awaking To More Pain

The anesthetic relief was short lived…I felt cheated! It felt like only a few moments of relief, then I was awake and in pain all over again. This time it was different yet again. The exploding sensations were gone and replaced with throbbing and aching all over my stomach, along with mental fog and delirium. I couldn't move or even shift at all without pain.

"The surgery was successful." I managed to comprehend that sentiment from someone in my loopy, half-conscious state.

I soon learned they had removed nearly my entire colon. The surgeon said about half of it was paper thin and watery and it nearly crumbled in his hand. Destroyed and irreparable. He had to remove it or I would not live.

He left the bottom 20 centimeters where it exits the body, and he just sewed that part shut and capped it off. His plan once I heal, to re-connect the small intestine to that portion. But meanwhile, the ostomy bag would be a permanent fixture for me unless they can successfully reconnect me later on.

Whatever works! As I became more coherent I felt immense gratitude for continued life, for no more explosive pain, and for a surgeon who had high confidence that I would truly heal. According to him, my problem had been resolved!

But I wasn't anywhere near being out of the woods. Supposedly 'healed' since they had removed my colon, the thought gave me hope momentarily. But why was I still in so much pain?

Oh yeah, major surgery. I forgot.

I guess it does take a toll on you when they slice open 8 inches of your stomach, remove 6 feet of deteriorating organs, sew your intestines to the wall of your stomach, and then re-connect it all with stitches and super glue. On top of the previous catastrophe, that made for a decent sized trauma to the body.

"OK, I can deal with that. I can accept that there is a recovery period I suppose." Thinking rationally and clearly on heavy doses of pain drugs and high trauma proved difficult. I learned later that Nan and some friends had been with me all afternoon after surgery, five or six hours. I vaguely remember any of it. They say I was out of it, sleeping on and off all afternoon. I'll have to take their word.

Certainly That Was A Bad Day Right?

That was definitely the most painful day of my life. I feel like I keep saying that. Do I keep saying that? Well, if so, it's because it's true. I was on a multi-month long escalator of pain that kept getting worse. Words cannot do justice to the pain I felt that day. Even trying to recount the experience I can't bring myself back to fully recall the feelings. It was the most horrific, frightening, painful thing I can imagine and thankfully I can't even get myself fully back there in memory. I don't wish that kind of pain or that kind of day on anyone.

But then again, maybe I do?

Not because I would ever wish harm on someone of course. But because of this reality that Napoleon Hill stated so eloquently: "Every adversity, every failure, and every heartache, carries with it the seed of an equivalent or greater benefit."

That was by a huge magnitude the most painful and challenging day of my life, and I was deeply convinced then, and still am today, that amazing benefits were bound to come because of it. I knew from all the previous tests and struggles that no matter what pain came, even if it produced death, I wouldn't choose to consider it bad for me. And I highly encourage you to choose the same. Because the greater the adversity the more amazing the potential benefits. And that awareness has produced immense amounts of joy and peace for me, and continues to do so.

That was not a bad day. A hard day? You bet! The hardest I could ever recall. But bad? Emphatically NO!! And I'm here to tell you and anyone who will listen, that there is no benefit to classifying days as 'bad'. We can find good and bad, positive and negative, in literally everything. Often it's hard to see the good right in the moment. But that doesn't mean it doesn't exist. Just like each ion has a positive and negative, the same is true for everything in life. And we are free to choose what we focus on.

When we label an entire day as bad we're closing our mind off to all the potential good and in the process inviting ourselves to feel down and discouraged. This may seem like a trivial matter, but words and thoughts are powerful. It's much more empowering to say, "this has been an intensely difficult day, so there must be some amazing lessons, blessings, or breakthroughs now available to me. I'm grateful for this pain and difficulty that has now opened up so many possibilities for pleasure and joy that didn't exist before."

When we say 'that was a bad day', we are unconsciously choosing to reject the potential good by focusing our attention on the negative. In the process we close ourselves off from looking for the good in our current situation. And we tend to find what we are looking for. So why choose to look for the bad when we obviously don't want more negative in our life?

Just look at all the good that came from the events of that day! I can choose to see the day as bad because I lost my colon and I will never get it back in this life. Or I can choose to see it as good because that surgeon saved my life that day and allowed me to continue living for another day, and being with my family, and having the potential of experiencing more joy on this mortal journey. I can choose to view the pain I experienced as bad for me, because it was so uncomfortable, annoying, discouraging, frightening, etc, etc. Or I can choose to see it as good for me, because now I have lived through an experience that will enable me to love and serve others in ways that were not even possible before. The pain is the necessary catalyst for me to experience the joy and fulfillment in this life that I truly want.

Acknowledging the intensity of the challenge and your fears, disappointments and failings is important! It's not helpful to hide from challenges, put blinders on and pretend everything is hunky dory all the time. That's not positive thinking, that's delusion. But accepting the pain, and choosing to remember that amazing potential is contained in it all, moves us into a better feeling place.

It moves us out of despairing thoughts into the hopeful and optimistic.

So for me? There is no bad day!

But since I'm a thick-skulled human, apparently I still needed more proof.

Please Give Me Some Food

The next morning I felt extreme hunger, and all I could eat was 'grape juice cocktail' and chicken broth. Better than nothing I sipped it down with gratitude. It did little to satisfy my physical hunger, but my soul felt so good it hardly mattered. All day on Sunday I sipped on juice cocktail and broth and reveled at being alive and out of massive pain. The painkillers seemed to be doing their duty wonderfully, supposedly my problem had been resolved.

Nan wrote this on Facebook that day:

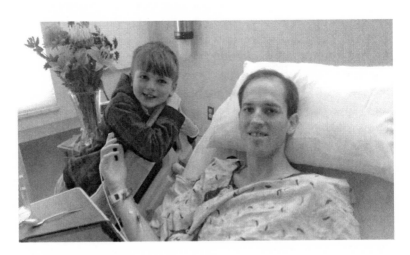

October 28, 2012

Today I am feeling grateful. Grateful that Aaron's life was spared. Grateful for a brilliant surgeon and alert, kind nurses watching over Aaron as he recovers from major surgery. Grateful for local friends and my church family who are supporting and serving us daily. Grateful for all the prayers and thoughts from loved ones. Thank you.

With visits from family and friends, and massively reduced pain, that Sunday was full of peace, hope, and optimism. The stark contrast to the prior 48 hours certainly enhanced how amazing it felt. Here's a Facebook post I made that day:

October 28, 2012

I have so much to be grateful for right now.

This smile may seem pretty weak still, but after yesterday it is the biggest smile ever.

Yesterday I went through more intense pain than ever before in my life, to the point where I literally didn't know if my body could survive it. After many hours of the intense pain I found myself asking the nurses/doctors if I was going to die. I desperately did not want to die, but not knowing what death felt like, I was totally unsure. I didn't know if at any moment something would just rupture and kill me. It was that intense and that painful.

Most painful day of my life. After surgery, a whole new host of surgery pains ensued.

But it was a very good day indeed.

Doctors are confident they fixed my issue and I will actually resume a normal life again now after recovering from the surgery.

And I am so grateful now to feel 90% better today than yesterday.

And I am so grateful to have such a bright hope of resuming my life once again, only now so much better off for having passed through this amazing challenge.

I am so thankful to God for giving me more life. I definitely do not feel ready to die, and I am so excited at the hope that it looks like I will be able to resume being the husband and father I was, and being there fully for my family again.

Of course I've got a little recovery to make. (May take me a bit longer to gain back the 40 pounds and energy lost.) But the path looks so much shorter today now that I know the problems have actually been removed.

So here's hoping for a quick, smooth recovery!

Thank you all for your continued prayers!

I am in awe at life. Life is truly amazing.

===============

Note: To get free access to the Truly Amazing Life Community and be motivated and inspired regularly go to: TrulyAmazingLife.com. As a member you will have access to tons of free helpful information and you will get first access to the products I create to help you live a Truly Amazing Life.

Life *is* truly amazing.

But the 'quick and smooth' parts of the recovery were not meant to be it turns out.

The next morning, October 29th, they allowed me to have a little bit of solid food. I thought I was making amazingly fast progress. I had some cream of wheat and yogurt in the morning. But within just a few hours, my stomach started cramping. I began feeling miserable. About that time Nan and my son Abe came in to visit. Abe would normally have been in school, but his stress, fear, and depression caused by my illness as well as other stressful situations with peers at school were manifesting as anxiety attacks and temper tantrums. Nan's intuitive compassion combined with her overwhelm in dealing with his emotional outbursts urged her to work out an agreement with Abe that she would take him out of school for the remainder of the semester in order to give him more attention and consider his best interest regarding school. His behavior threatened to cut the last emotional thread Nan was dangling by and her heart was telling her he just needed more love and security.

The spark that had been slowly eating away at the fuse, touching powder in a grand explosion two days prior, was about to reach a second pile of explosives...

KA-BOOM!!

I was in no position to be helping anyone in the state I was in. I could barely talk, let alone relate properly with people. I was certainly in no position to be effectively and lovingly parenting. But for some reason (the natural fathering instinct I suppose) I felt compelled to step in and help Nan discipline Abe that morning. Rather than helping though, my actions became the final straw to break the camel's back and initiated a tsunami of intense emotional suffering that assaulted me and most of my family, and felt like it would dash us all to pieces.

I was not my normal, capable self. Not only had I been distanced from what was going on with Abe for months due to my debilitating illness, I was now just two days out of major surgery and too consumed with my own healing to really focus on Abe's. The drugs, the pain, the starving, I had plenty of good reasons to not attempt parental discipline and just sit on the sidelines for a bit. Unfortunately, I didn't make that choice. I jumped right in the parenting game, injured and sick as I was.

Nan and Abe hadn't been there long at all when I asked Abe why he refused to go to school. "I hate school!" is about all we ever got out of him. A power struggling debate ensued. Abe defiantly stated that we can't force him to do anything and refused to go to school anymore. To which I responded that maybe we couldn't force him, but we certainly could take away all his privileges. With that threat, he made some threats of his own. If we took his things away he would purposefully make our life harder and do nothing we asked. My blood boiled as the tension rose and the struggle mounted. "How could he say such a cruel thing...seeing the condition his parents were both in?" I thought.

But he was obviously fighting for survival himself. The experience of watching his dad wither away and nearly die, completely change personalities, and virtually vanish as a father figure had highly traumatized him. But in the heat of that moment, I lashed back with something like "if you don't want to live by the rules of our house, then we'll just put you up for adoption and you can go live with someone else!"

Immediately he shoved his face into his mom's coat and started sobbing.

What did I just do?? Did I actually say that? Nan was visibly shocked and restrained herself from breathing fire back at me as she consoled Abe. She glared at me as if to say, "YOU DID NOT JUST SAY THAT!!!" I immediately recognized my mistake. I was trying to help but I clumsily and angrily hurt the people I loved most. Nan nearly burst into tears and couldn't stay. She picked up Kelsie, and with one more deserved look of disgust and resentment toward me, shuffled Abe out the door.

I wanted to crawl into a hole and die.

Mortified, I couldn't believe I had said such a mean thing to my son in that commanding, cruel way. There was no love in my action, only pain, fear and an attempt to somehow force something to change. I had just dropped an atomic bomb on my family that would prove the cause of intense suffering and pain for us all. I sobbed in my bed uncontrollably, every ounce of remaining energy consumed by deep regret.

I had just wounded my son's heart. My only son whom I loved so much and was so scared and fragile. I had treated him with utter contempt and hatred. And I had spit in the face of my angel wife, Nan. She had been trying so hard to be loving and compassionate to the children and I let her down in the very moment she needed more support than ever. Now my heart threatened to explode. Come on! I thought we were past the explosions?

Extinction Can Be Enticing

Within an hour after they left, my abdomen and remaining intestines launched into an intense cramp session. My bowels completely locked down like they were knotting up around themselves in a permanent contraction. Intense nausea set in and tormented me for the next four to five hours. I begged the nurse for some relief...some drug...something to stop the intense pain. But the pain killers weren't stopping any of the pain. Sweating and moaning, my heart agonized and despaired over the pain I just caused my family.

Physical torture combined with emotional despair. I had no faith or positive thinking reserves left to pull me through this time. I felt like I was nothing. I thought it might consume me. I wished it would in fact. I wished I could somehow stop existing.

But I couldn't cease existing of course, so I suffered. Finally after hours of nauseous cramping pain I started puking. But every convulsion felt like a knife slicing open the eight inch incision in my stomach from surgery. Thankfully the stitches and glue held firm. I vaguely recall 5 or 6 people in my room trying to clean and help me. I was in a daze, moaning in pain, with puke everywhere.

Soon someone decided I needed a tube in my nose to pump out my stomach. They tried jamming it in my right nostril, thwarted by my screaming and thrashing. The left nostril brought even more screaming and thrashing. Back to the right nostril demanding that I hold still. Someone please have mercy on me!!

Finally they forced the tube in my right nostril and the agony ended. Within 20 minutes the pain, bloating, and cramping went down dramatically. Thank you. Thank you. A reprieve. I can breathe. But, oh wait…now I can think again. I don't want to think! No!!

That night nothing consoled me. I was not wondering how this might turn out to benefit me, far from it. I had cracked. Reason, logic, and hope had left the building. Enshrouded by a thick blackness of regret and self-loathing, and feeling run over by the physical torture, I hated myself. Something I had not felt for a long, long time. So disappointed in my action, I wished so badly I could take it back it was nearly unbearable. I wished to be extinct. Being alive was just too painful to fathom anymore.

Begging Forgiveness

I wallowed in self-loathing, but it couldn't last. I couldn't die. I couldn't vanish. I already shed every tear inside me. All that remained was to act.

I called Nan to apologize, but she wasn't answering. I left an apology message, begging for her forgiveness. And I waited, and prayed for a response. Something to let me know she was OK. That we were OK. But nothing came. In the past, she always responded to my texts. We never let things go longer than a day. But not this time. I checked my phone all night. I shivered at the fears that I had destroyed our relationship permanently somehow. Sleepless fits and nightmares that my family left me consumed the night.

Thankfully, day follows night. And light dispels darkness. As the sun rose on the next morning, my physical pain had vanished. And along with the light of the day, a small ray of hope lit my soul when I saw this email from Nan. It turns out neither of us slept that night:

From: Nan Kennard
Sent: Tuesday, October 30, 2012 3:23 AM
To: Aaron Kennard
Subject: Abe

I am sorry to report but our son has now spiraled down into full on self-deprecating, weeping, bawling, self-blamed depression. I know you think he just needs to change his thoughts and I need to expect him to but I also know from personal experience exactly how he is feeling and I refuse to continue to follow your suggestion to crack down and take things away from him and expect him to just rise up and be a man today. He has already had so much taken away from him and is mourning the loss of the happy, patient, gentle father he once had.

He needs love, patience, understanding and peace. I am trying SO hard to give that to him and I am sorry if you feel like I am sabotaging him. I am trying my best to follow the Spirit and to love Abe in God's way. Abe told me he feels like he doesn't matter and no one cares about how he is feeling. He wishes you would stay in the hospital longer because you were mean and angry and he is afraid you have become that way forever.

I think you need to keep focused on healing yourself and I will keep trying to not stress you with all the crap going on at home. I know we will get through this eventually but I am not delusional in thinking it is going away tonight. If God is telling me to take Abe out of school for a while, don't you dare tell me I am wrong and I am spoiling him. You have no idea the full extent of what is going on because you have been so consumed with your own pain and suffering lately and believe me I don't blame you. You have been through Hell and back and I am sorry for how trying that has been. We are in Hell, too. And it sucks.

So I may just have to hold Abe near me for a while and cry with him because frankly I am depressed, too, and I am sick and tired of fighting with Abe and taking away the last few things that bring him peace. I can't sleep through this pain and I need Abe to love me rather that hate me for punishing him for feelings he is not actually as in control of as you may think. You work on yourself and I will work on me and Abe.

I love you and I know you'll be yourself again soon. Keep being strong and optimistic. I will be strong and optimistic, too. I am sorry I don't do things the way you think I should but at least I am standing by you. I am pretty sure other women would have crumbled under this weight weeks ago. But I am still standing by you, praying for and envisioning your healthy return.

Yours in Faith,
Nan

My wife is amazing! I am so blessed to have such a strong, faith-filled, patient woman as a companion. I don't know of anything in life that compares to the feeling of loving companionship. Those words of faith and support relieved my tension significantly. But the injury remained. I had clearly hurt my son and hurled him farther down the path of depression. It stung fiercely to think on it. I wrote this in reply:

From: Aaron Kennard
Sent: Tuesday, October 30, 2012 6:56 AM
To: Nan Kennard
Subject: Re: Abe

Thanks, Nan. I will defer to your judgment in following the spirit on it.

That was clearly a poor way to handle things by me yesterday and I'm so sorry. I will do my best to make it up to Abe, and you.

It should have been between you and me in a place of me listening and trying to understand the situation a lot better.

I love you and support you and know God will guide you as to what is best. You really are amazing, so strong, and are a literal angel to me. I am so sorry for the harm and setback I caused.

Yesterday, right as you left initiated 12 hours of Hell for me.

All the food I ate that morning and afternoon began a torture bloating session on my bowels. It turned into the next 4-5 hours of me tossing/turning and trying through intense wound wrenching stomach pain, to puke.

Medicine after med, pain killer, Zofran, anti-nausea,

nothing working. Finally at 9 or 10 PM I had 5 staff working on me trying to figure it out.

And somehow miraculously I puked finally, kind of a lot. It was Hell, though. And then it got worse. They had to ram a plastic tube down my nose into my stomach to suction
everything out. It's still there. I have slept maybe an hour tonight through major hiccups. Hours later it is still sucking out bile. But hugely relieving is the stomach cramps and bloating are gone.

I love you,
Aaron

Her email eased my agony, but all day I called and texted with no response, desperately waiting in silent torture for a call from Nan. Finally, hearing her voice that evening brought immediate tears and relief. After she called I sent this email to my son:

From: Aaron Kennard
Sent: Tuesday, October 30, 2012 6:31 PM
To: Abe Kennard
Subject: I'm so sorry.

My Dear son Abe,

I'm so sorry about the harsh words I spoke to you yesterday. I wish I could take the whole conversation back, but I can't.

I love you, Abe. And I want you to be happy. And I want to be the loving father you deserve.

I am very sick right now and I am having a hard time being the dad you deserve. That is not your fault. But

I will get better, and I will be there for you again.

You are such an amazing son, Abe. I'm so proud of you and so grateful to be in your family.

I know our Heavenly Father will help you and me, and Mom and the girls through this tough time.

God loves you. He loves us.

And I ask you to please forgive me for not speaking to you as loving as God would have yesterday. Please know that you can always turn to your Heavenly Father in prayer for comfort, even when your earthly father is struggling. God never struggles, He is perfect and He is always there for us.

I love you, Abe!

My heart ached all day for Abe. Nan was strong enough to understand I was not myself and I didn't mean harm. She could cope with it somewhat. But Abe was now fully depressed and despondent because of my actions. The weight of guilt and shame pressed down and covered me all day with claustrophobic anxiety. I just hoped that my email could comfort him somehow.

Later that evening Nan and I exchanged some texts confirming her love and support and telling Abe was touched and forgiving.

Wow!! Life is a rollercoaster! And I think Winston Churchill gave the best possible advice to follow during the Hell portions of the ride:

"If you're going through Hell, keep going!"

Chapter 7

Clawing Out Of The Pit

Still Starving

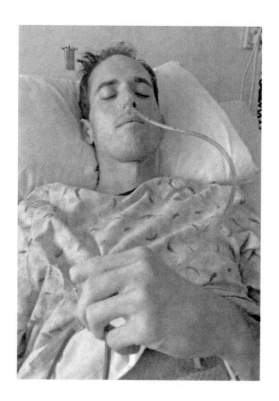

I wonder, is starving worse than drowning? I don't know for sure, but I would guess it is. Because drowning can only last a couple minutes, and starving can go on for days and weeks even! It's a horrible feeling to be deteriorating and feeling your body starving to death. But after the epic failure of an attempt to eat solid foods, I had reverted to no food at all. Not even liquid calories. Nothing. I couldn't bring myself to eat. The fear of pain from eating trumped the pain of starving. I didn't get any substantial food into my system for over a week.

On Halloween, they stopped the stomach suction and I drank a cup of apple juice. I immediately cramped so they started the suction again. Looks like the tube is staying in! On the plus side, at least I got to be 'Crazy tube in the face man!' for Halloween (As Adam Sandler would have no doubt called me.)

I had been begging for nutrition through an IV. I couldn't last forever on a diet of ice chips. Yet despite my obvious pain and inability to eat, the doctors hesitated prescribing it for some reason. Finally on Wednesday Nan convinced them, but they wouldn't start the nutrition until the following night at 9 PM. GROAN!!! How could I survive another day without any nutrition?

Apparently we can survive longer than we think on just liquid. But it's no fun I assure you. My energy neared empty when a group of eight of my friends came to visit. So nice to see them, and feel their support and love, but when they asked how they could help, I could only point to my wife's phone number on the white board. Speaking was agony. So tired. So drained. I lived solely on the hope of the 9 PM arrival of nutrients.

Finally the nutrition bag came, they plugged it in and I went to sleep.

Weighing In

I slept in peace that night, and felt some hope now that I finally had IV nutrition and my bowels could rest. The next day I could feel the energy filling me up, like someone had plugged me in to an electric socket to recharge. Such a huge relief!

My weight registered at 131 pounds that day. Though I did feel much better suddenly, the road to recovery seemed to stretch off into the distance forever with no end in sight. But I took solace in the hope that I was legitimately on that road now!

I took this self-portrait with my phone that day after they removed the heinous nose tube.

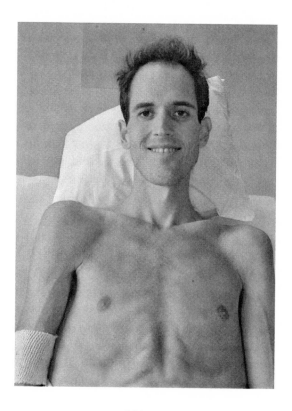

Little more than skin and bone, most of my muscles severely atrophied. Barely able to walk to the bathroom, and I could only manage that at most once a day. Otherwise, the nurses emptied my ostomy bag and my portable urinal for me and I just lay there. But I felt happy. So grateful to have the nose tube removed, the nutrition pumping in, and my wife's forgiveness. What a relief!! Here's what Nan wrote on Facebook that day:

November 2, 2012 – Nan Kennard

The past few days have been rough. Aaron's stomach is still not accepting any food, not even juice or jello. He has a stomach pump in all the time now to help alleviate the cramping. His color is not great either as he is super anemic.

The docs finally started him on total parenteral nutrition (IV) last night so he is getting a 24 hour drip of 3,000 calories with fat, protein, carbs, and vitamins customized to exactly what his body needs after looking at his deficiencies via blood test. Thank goodness for that!! We were asking for that in the hospital two weeks ago before the whole perforating colon ordeal, but the docs wouldn't give it to us then because he hadn't been starving for long enough and they wanted to keep giving his bowels a chance to start digesting.

Apparently losing 40 lbs in 6 weeks is not starving long enough. What? Anyway, here we are now post surgery and the docs say it's quite common for the digestion to take its time working again after removing the large bowel and not to worry yet. A few days on IV nutrition and he'll try food again.

Aaron's mental outlook is still quite good despite his exhaustion, weakness and pain. He has been a solid rock of strength and optimism throughout all of this. Every time I visit I feel uplifted and hopeful. If anyone wants to go visit him he is still in Boulder Community Hospital on Broadway. He could use as many happy smiles and words of encouragement as he can get. Thanks for your continued faith and prayers on our

*behalf. And thanks to all of those who have brought meals,
watched my kids, and carried me through this challenging time.*

Thankfully Nan is super optimistic and was already forgetting about her dreadful visit with me on Monday, where she definitely did not "feel uplifted and hopeful". My daughter Breanne further enhanced my mood, still beautiful even with a huge nose and no front teeth. She brings joy to my soul no matter how I am feeling.

What Matters More?

There is no way I could list all the amazing acts of love and selfless service that were extended to me and my family during this time. Each act was immensely appreciated, and gave me energy to continue forward. This experience opened my eyes to just how loving and compassionate people are inherently. Daily I received calls, visits, emails, and expressions of love and concern.

One particularly poignant and touching act of love came from a close friend who was and is still dealing with his own chronic, intense pain with accompanied full body convulsions at least every other day. He had already suffered over 18 months and there was no end in sight for him. His undiagnosed ailment had completely changed his lifestyle from active and always going, to almost no energy and always suffering pain.

But despite his constant pain, this loving man who I will always call a true friend was in the hospital with me nearly every day for the entire week after my surgery. He would massage my calves and feet giving such relief to the atrophied muscles. He read scripture and words of life and positivity bringing me hope and reminding me of the truth. An amazing blessing in my time of need, I could hardly believe he had the energy to do that for me. Love in the purest sense, it taught me a new meaning to the word. I will be forever grateful to him for his compassion. More than anyone else, this friend truly understood my pain. I hope to become more like him, he set an example for me to follow the rest of my life.

I think his love for me, and the compassion and service from so many others, contributed to this dream and a blog post I wrote about it on November 6th:

TrulyAmazingLife.com
November 6, 2012
What Matters More?

Last night was a really rough night for me.

After being able to eat throughout the day and feeling decent, my bowels started majorly cramping just before bedtime.

Then the heartburn and hiccups kicked in. A couple strong narcotics took the edge off just a bit, but it was a long and painful night to say the least. And the suffering gets compounded at night when it becomes a mental battle of discouragement in addition to the pain, as my mind naturally wants to know when the setbacks are going to ever stop. At this point I don't know when I'm going to be able to go home from the hospital...it feels like I have so far to go sometimes.

But here is something I am grateful for last night that I want to share.

I had a dream....

It was late in the day and my family had made the last order of food at a convention of some type. The kids were all hungry and ready to go home. We were tired.

When our food order was placed on the warming table I didn't get to it until another rather large family had already arrived on the scene and began to claim it.

Matter-of-factly and hurriedly I informed them that was our order and I proceeded to gather all the food and usher my family into the adjoining cafeteria room.

As I closed the door on them after successfully 'protecting my little flock' of a family and getting all of our food, I saw the dejected looks on their children's faces and noticed the family wasn't going to get any food because everything was closed and that was the last of it.

As I sat down to eat, I immediately started bawling. I was so ashamed of myself. I ran back out the door in tears in my dream and begged the man to forgive me and to come and share our food with us. The fact is we had plenty and probably more than we were going to eat anyway.

Their whole family with 4 or 5 kids came in and we shared a meal, and some tears, laughter, and hugs.

I woke up from the dream in tears.

Not from the pain in my chest or my bowels, but from a heart full of the joy felt from service and forgiveness and compassion.

I hoped I could live while I was awake with compassion also, and not just in my dreams.

Then in the morning after that really long night, my angel wife came in to see me early at about 8 am.

I was discouraged and still in pain. And I was trying not to be negative but it was really, really, REALLY hard.

But Nan managed to pull me out of it with her bright spirit, her love, and her compassion. And my goal the rest of the day has been to brighten those around me with at least a smile, and a kind word, regardless of how I'm feeling.

Life is too short to live it without loving. I'm grateful to be learning these lessons more deeply through this intense trial. I am finding joy every day, even amidst a lot of pain sometimes.

And really, what is the point of it all if we are not showing love to others in some way?

I can't see one.

Let's live today like it's Truly Amazing! (Because it is;)

-Aaron

Life had turned into such an emotional rollercoaster that the new normal was fluctuating many times daily between tears of joy and tears of sadness. Even though I was filled with so much joy, hope and feelings of love that day, the pain never fully left, always grinding away at me.

Getting Discharged

Living life in a hospital leaves much to be desired: all day in a reclining bed, never changing out of a hospital robe, showering only occasionally due to the pain and hassle of it all, staring at the same wall for weeks on end, looking up at a blank TV that I refused to turn on because it could only possibly elicit depression.

And the food! Terrible! Repetitive and ironically super low quality. You would think a place of healing would put at least some focus on healing foods, but definitely not. Even my surgeon acknowledged this irony.

The nurses I had the privilege of being served by were amazing though. Their tender, loving service, blessed me day and night. On the night before they sent me home, one of my nurses compassionately talked me off a ledge of insanity for over an hour at 2 in the morning. I woke up at about 1:30 AM sweating and filled with anxiety, in the middle of a horrible nightmare. I dreamt I had woken up with a major setback, everything going completely wrong. My bowels locked down again and I would not be able to go home. Petrified because everything was worse than ever and I would stay in the hospital indefinitely since there was no solution.

As I woke up in the same place as my dream I couldn't distinguish dream from reality. I kept checking myself to see if I was in pain, but I couldn't tell because the dream seemed so real. I called for the nurse. "Am I OK? I can't tell. Can I still go home? I feel like everything is horribly wrong!" I panicked.

After giving me more pain meds, my nurse sat by my bed and just talked to me. I asked her if she could stay because I couldn't tell if I was dreaming. She assured me I was awake and just fine, but I couldn't quite believe it. So she stayed and we just talked for over an hour. I learned of her family, and her background, and how much she adores her now grown up children. And how much passion and love she has for being a nurse. I told her of my background, and we discussed philosophies on living happily. The anxiety left and I fell back asleep. Just another example of a loving act I will never forget. People are so good!

That morning after nearly two weeks holed up in my hospital room, I couldn't have been more thrilled when Nan picked me up and took me home! Seeing my house, my kids, and their welcome home sign filled my soul. Still moving slow, barely walking, and only weighing 130 pounds, but I was home!!

Jumping The Gun

The 'felt so good to be home' part swiftly faded unfortunately. I went straight to my bed to lie down when I got home. Nan fed me some chicken, rice and veggies in bed. And not an hour later my stomach locked up on me again with cramps. "Oh, no! Not again!" I attempted narcotics to relieve the pain, but nothing worked. It got worse and worse as the evening progressed. Writhing in pain and thrashing around all over the bed moaning.

Nan called the doctor in panic. "It should go away," he said. "See if you can make it through the night, this should pass. Call me if it gets worse."

It got worse. Extreme nausea started its night-shift of torture. 5 hours of agony later at 1:30 AM after barely sleeping at all, a painful and gut wrenching puke fest ensued; somewhat relieving, but totally exhausting. Now totally dehydrated, I staggered into our tiny master bathroom. I recall leaning over the toilet to grab a plastic bucket. Then the next thing I remember is coming to consciousness on my back to Nan screaming at the top of her lungs for help.

She had watched mortified from our bed as my skeletal frame collapsed in a thud against the wall, eyes wide open, mouth gaping, and completely unconscious. The image apparently gave her nightmares for weeks afterwards. Frantically she pulled me to the floor as she screamed for her mom in our guest bedroom. They called 911 and literally less than 60 seconds later EMT's were in my bedroom, they just happened to be right around the corner.

I was loaded on a stretcher and hauled off to the ER again. This time, my three older children, all awake in our front room, looked on in shock and fear as they wheeled me into the frigid night. My heart ached to see the fear in their eyes, and nothing I could do. I longed to hold them, to cry with them, to comfort them. But they were gone. And I was on my way back to the emergency room for the fourth time in a five week period. That morning Nan wrote on Facebook:

November 9, 2012

Well, I guess we jumped the gun. After 12 hours of excruciating bowel pain and finally puking up everything he ate yesterday and scaring the living daylights out of me by passing out in the bathroom, here we are back at Boulder Community Hospital for a few more days.

129

Amazing Experiences with Love and Grace

Now back in the hospital depression blurred the days and negativity bombarded me. I didn't want to see anyone. But I knew I needed help to get out of my head. One morning some loving friends came and I nearly chewed them out for just smiling when I felt so angry at my lot in life. Thankfully they patiently stayed over an hour. The light of their presence pulled me out of the darkness. Another day I wrote this on Facebook:

November 12, 2012

As a quick update...I went home from the hospital less than a day last week and I'm back in, working on my degree in ultimate patience as I continue to somehow survive the hospital liquid diet and slowly allow my stomach and bowels to start cooperating again.

Last night I had an amazing love-filled spiritual experience with my dad which I am so grateful for...and it continues to prove to me that there can always be good and even amazing found in each day. So, even if I am bombarded today with challenge, pain, boredom, negative thoughts or whatever, I'm going to do my best to keep looking for something amazing about today. I assure you it is no easy task some days. But what better course of action is there?

-Aaron

P.S. - Count your blessings. If your body is functioning normally be grateful, it is such a gift to have a healthy body.

Really, what better course is there than to seek the good in it all?

Amidst moments of dark despair, my father and I grew closer that night than I had ever felt before. We held each other, cried together, and prayed together. My heart filled with peace as I knew somehow the pain would pass, though I still didn't see the way. I felt total comfort in the arms of my father, relying completely upon his love and compassion. I felt through him the tender love of my Heavenly Father. I sobbed in gratitude to God for giving me this new ray of hope in my darkness. My pain and problems were consumed and meaningless in the presence of the light, peace, and joy I felt in my hospital room for an hour that Sunday night.

Other nights Nan crawled into my hospital bed, holding me, crying with me, listening to my fears and concerns, assuring me we would make it through. I ached each time she left me there. She was always so patient, so loving, and so tender. Despite crawling through Hell herself, confronted with fears and nightmares of my death and becoming a widow. Despite my irritability. Despite her son losing control of his mind and emotions. Despite feeling lost, out of control, and barely hanging on to hope herself. Overwhelmed and constantly on the verge of cracking from the weight of it all, yet still patient with me. And she had her own tender moments of peace as she fed Kelsie and looked into the eyes of her newborn daughter who was oblivious of the storm raging all around her. Just at peace. A small piece of heaven and a saving grace for Nan helping pull her through. Reminding her of God's love. Bringing eternal perspective, which brought just enough peace to see her through a few more hours.

Finally Home to Stay

After another full week of severely depressing lows and amazing spiritual highs in the hospital, November 14th I finally came home for good. And I actually had enough energy to sit at the table and play cards with my son and my dad! Still in the mid 130's though, and looking pretty skeletal. Abe was happy that day. He said he had forgiven me, but he was far from recovered from the trauma that had decimated his emotions. I wrote this on Facebook the next week:

November 19, 2012

I finally got to come home from the hospital last Wednesday. It is SO good to be home. My strength is coming back and my digestive system is a little better each day. It's so relieving to finally be seeing some progress.

This afternoon I went out with Nan and ate a Larkburger and strawberry shake that I was craving. Then we went to REI to get me some clothes. I almost felt like a normal human being again...which was pretty cool.

Last night I was able to tuck my kids in to bed for the first time in months. It was such a sweet experience, and it felt so good to finally be able to help and take some of the load off of Nan. She deserves some kind of award for what she has been through with a newborn, 3 extremely needy and scared kids, and an incapacitated husband the last few months. I am so blessed to be married to such a strong woman...her ability to endure hardship is mind boggling.

I am thankful to all of you that have been praying, and sending positive energy our way. And especially thankful for the many people that have been supporting Nan and coming with food and help with the kids and the house. We have received so much kindness and help. I've still got a lot of recovery and I'm 40 pounds underweight. I'm still on IV nutrition to supplement at night. But I'm home and things are getting better each day and I'm grateful to God beyond description to be back with my family instead of stuck in a hospital bed alone all day.

Emotional Trauma

Things improved it seemed, though slowly. But there were setbacks. Each day was different, and our son's mental well-being brought constant anxiety.

The trauma of my illness, and the emotional distress my words had caused that day in the hospital, created severe repercussions with my son. He was not his normal, happy, bright, and loving self, and I still felt weight from some of the responsibility for that. Nan and I cried together every night with broken hearts over our son's mental state. Somewhere deep inside there was hope he

133

would recover, but when? He had totally changed. He was suffering so badly that he was barely recognizable to us.

He was at home all day since Nan had pulled him out of school, and we lived on pins and needles. Nan became too scared to leave him in his room alone after finding him lying face down in a small pool of his own blood apathetic to the fact that his nose was bleeding all over the place after hitting his head against the carpet.

He told us many times that he wanted to be dead. It seemed he couldn't see anything good about being alive. His face and body were often lifeless, the brightness dimmed in his eyes. He often hid underneath his hoodie or sulked around the house with his blanket draped over him. He could be distracted from his despair for short periods of time and we would get a glimpse of his true self but as soon as the external stimulus was gone, he would sink back into sadness. We were in turmoil with no idea how to help him.

My continued pain and bloating on top of all this threatened to sever the remaining strands of emotional stability for both Nan and me. We were both in and out of emotional break downs and depression ourselves. Generally I felt OK, because just being out of my prison cell of a hospital room was enough to bring me some happiness whenever I thought about it. The contrast and beauty of just being in the presence of my family, despite the emotional issues, compared to the solitary confinement of the hospital brightened my spirit daily. But the magnitude of the bleakness of our situation still blocked most of the light. We could not see an end to the tunnel of suffering we were groping our way through.

Some part of me knew we would see light at some point, even though there was no visible evidence to suggest it. I still believed this was happening for our good. But how could this be good? I'm alive, but doomed to constant and ever changing pain? And what has happened to my innocent son?

I've found that a key to faith is forgetting the 'how'. The how doesn't matter. It is irrelevant in fact. And becoming good at forgetting the 'how', is precisely 'how' to make it through tough times. Worrying about things that are impossible to see in the moment is useless and detrimental. I knew without any shred of doubt that all these things were somehow for my good. I had come to believe that there can be no other way than that, because God would not exist, and therefore I would not exist if it were any different. So I didn't have to question that premise. And if that premise is true, that every single thing that happens to us is for our ultimate good, then it doesn't really matter 'how' it's going to work out. I can rest my mind knowing that somehow it will. Trusting that even though I don't see the way, and even though it may look impossible from my perspective, that God sees it all, and knows exactly what I need to have joy and ultimate happiness. I can't see everything that is coming around the next bend, nor would it be good if I could.

The Radar Screen

The amount of possibilities in life we can see or even imagine is like a radar screen on a ship. There are countless things happening across the ocean, but in our ship all we see beyond our immediate proximity is what shows up on our tiny little radar screen. We can't see much, a fraction of one percent of everything going on in the vast ocean. But that doesn't mean things aren't on their way into our view soon. It's the same in life, as we move forward, new things, people, and circumstances will show up that we could have never even imagined, because they were off our radar screen. But they will be the very things we need to solve many of our challenges.

We don't know how it's all going to work out. But it always will. We don't have to worry about how things are going to happen. The 'how' is almost always off our radar screen. We just have to trust our feelings, given to us by our creator. He knows exactly what we need and when we need it. Everything that has shown up is for our good. We can learn from it and benefit from it all in some way. And we can feel the things off our radar screen, even when we can't see them. Certainly God sees everything coming our way, and we can learn to be guided by Him through our feelings, rather than only trusting what we see. **"For we walk by faith, not by sight."** (2 Corinthians 5:7)

So how was Abe being intensely depressed, disturbed, and sad beneficial for him or us?

I don't know. I don't claim to know how it all works. But I still believe that good will come from it. And even though it was the last thing on earth we could have wanted, there is some benefit to be gained from having experienced it...for him and for us.

The week of Thanksgiving brought reprieve, support, and service. Three of my sisters and their entire family's came to be with us, literally giving us the strength to carry on. The distraction of having cousins in town to play with was heaven to both Abe and to us. He got lost in play and became mostly content. Whew!!! How desperately we needed that reprieve. The emotional support from loving siblings recharged our souls.

Chapter 8

The Truth Shall Set You Free

An Endless Recovery Loop

Thanksgiving week as the kids were out of school, I actually ventured out to a movie with the family and shopping with Nan. Wow, a taste of normal life! But it was not normal of course. I still had toxic gas and intense bloating coming and going. And the gas was coming out both ends. But since the end exiting my stomach was contained in a bag that was not a huge social issue. Unfortunately for everyone involved, there was no containing the toxic gas coming up out of my mouth. There is nothing that can describe the nastiness of the burps that were bursting forth, other than toxic gas. I tried to hold them in, but it was no use. They could not be stopped. And on the way home from the movie theater the kids were all groaning and moaning in pain from the stench which instantly filled every crevice of our minivan. I would have felt bad for them if I weren't nearly dying from it myself. Windows down, freezing winter air blowing in was the only way we could survive the drive.

But even still, I was home! I was with my family! My wife and kids were glad to have me home and tried to stay lighthearted and optimistic about my new ostomy and toxic burps. I even saw "Dad's toxic burps" show up in a couple of their gratitude journals one night as we laughed and joked about my "healing." Certainly this had to pass sometime. But how?? And when? It had already been a month since the surgery and I was still having major intestinal and digestive issues. They told me they had "removed the problem" when they removed my diseased colon! Well, my problems were clearly not removed. And that was highly disconcerting to me.

Nan and I discussed frequently whether or not I had been diagnosed correctly. We wondered, and worried a bit, whether I actually had Crohn's disease and not just ulcerative colitis. The doctors were 99% sure I just had UC and that the surgery was "curative". They love to cure things with surgery! Isn't it great?! We can just cut the bad part out and you're healed...hurray!!

Ummm....OK, doc. What about the fact that there is a reason why I got this disease in the first place?? Any idea what that reason may be? And did we solve the root cause of the issue, or did we just chop out the symptom?

"Well....nobody knows for sure. It's a complex issue. So many variables! It's most likely a genetic issue. Food definitely plays no factor in the cause of your issue. There is no proof that diet has anything to do with it. We do know that we have cured the UC now by removing your colon."

It seemed more and more apparent to me that my problems were not gone and my body was not "cured". But I kept holding on to the hope that the doctors were right, and it would pass, and I would be OK eventually. Meanwhile I was still in pain! I couldn't sleep at night without taking narcotics to dull the stomach cramping.

Thanksgiving Day came and we enjoyed a delicious meal prepared by my siblings. But sure enough, that evening after eating too much food, and definitely too much of that delicious Marie Calendar's chocolate mousse cream pie, the bowel pain set in severely. More bloating. More toxic burps and gas. More narcotics to try to sleep.

I tossed and turned in my rented hospital bed and woke up frequently. Wondering if I would ever heal. Wishing I could sleep in my own bed again with Nan. Still hooked to an IV for nutrition and liquid each night. At least by now I figured out how to remove the IV tubes each morning by myself, using my teeth. A huge success of independence and a step toward freedom! But am I ever going to recover from this?

A Doctor Who Can Heal

Back in September a good friend had referred me to his 'magic miracle worker doctor'. He raved about how the guy miraculously knew the solutions to his family's health challenges. Every one of his treatments brought satisfactory results. He was over the top in his testimonial of the man. I was easily convinced.

I was desperate at the time and open to anything in October. The traditional, insurance- covered medical community wasn't helping me. But the first time George's doc could get me in, I couldn't make my appointment. I had gone to the ER and was stuck in the hospital in mid-October. I rescheduled. Then during the next appointment I was nearly unconscious recovering from major surgery in another hospital. The stars weren't lining up, but I felt pulled to see this doctor. Finally the day after Thanksgiving I was able to keep my appointment with Dr. Lundell.

A Transformational Day

November 23, 2012 I left Dr. Lundell's office with a huge bag of natural supplements, a very long receipt for blood tests, stool tests, and the doc's time, and nearly $2000 less available credit on my card. "Well, that was an expensive kick in the pants!" I thought, since natural cure doctors are not covered by most insurance. "Thanks, George!"

Here's the gist of how the visit went down:

Dr. Lundell: They did not 'cure' you by removing your colon. You will continue to have problems and pain throughout your life, and you'll inevitably be back in the hospital for more surgeries if you don't change your diet dramatically.

Me: Umm…Uhh…OK? Are you sure?

Dr: Yes. Your problem is not just genetic. And it definitely was not just contained to your colon. There's a reason why you're still in massive pain, bloating, and gas, beyond just recovering from surgery.

Me: Do tell!

He proceeded to lecture me for about 90 minutes on how my immune and digestive system works, and on the reason why I got the disease in the first place.

FINALLY!!! A physical person in the medical field who will actually admit there is a cause to this stuff! You have no idea how refreshing it was to hear this, and at the same time daunting and completely overwhelming. He confirmed everything I had read in many books, which the medical doctors all dismissed as 'anecdotal'. And my feelings told me Dr. Lundell knew exactly what he was talking about, and that he was right.

He told me the reason why different types of foods stress the digestive and immune system and why they are large contributors to all auto-immune diseases and disorders. He confirmed that the causes are indeed complex and many, and that genetics does play a role in what part of the body is weaker or more prone to attack. But in no uncertain terms he showed me that emotional stressors as well as physical stressors are at the root of the cause of all auto-immune problems. And he showed me why the food we put in our digestive tract is one of the largest of those stressors. There are many books and studies on this topic, so I won't even attempt to go into much detail here because I wouldn't do it justice. I will just stick to the basics of what he told me and share with you what happened to me.

In a nutshell, he educated me in general, and then he told me specifically what I should and should absolutely NOT be eating. He told me in no uncertain terms that I should not be going anywhere near wheat, anything with gluten, all dairy products, all refined sugar, and a bunch of other inflammatory foods such as peanuts and anything in the nightshade family (tomatoes, eggplant, peppers, etc.). And he told me I should eat only organic foods, and only the highest quality meats that were grass fed, organic, and/or wild caught. And eat absolutely nothing that had been made with genetically modified ingredients. Then he prescribed a bunch of supplements including digestive enzymes to aid in the absorption of nutrients, probiotics to help restore good bacteria, and natural anti-inflammatory substances like Aloe and others to aid in healing.

Nan and I were together at the appointment, and his extreme education and recommendations had left us both stunned, bewildered, and in a state of sticker shock. We had already maxed out our $10,000 medical insurance deductible for the year.

But we felt he spoke the truth. And he backed it up with nearly a ream of literature that he sent me with for homework. But it was such hard truth! I wanted to believe the medical doctors! Their way seemed so much easier and more convenient. I wanted to keep eating Belgian waffles smeared with butter and maple syrup, fruit and whipped cream! I wanted to eat pizza, and a juicy burger and French fries! I wanted to eat ice cream and strawberry milkshakes, dangit!!! Am I now doomed to never eating what I want ever again? The thought was overwhelming. What about caramels and dark chocolate? Certainly I could eat those in moderation right? Nope. Not according to Dr. Lundell. I wanted to cry. I wanted to crawl in a hole and hibernate. It was daunting for Nan, as well.

One of the first things he said to us was: "Sugar is poison." And he meant it. "There is no place in your life for refined sugar. It is a toxic substance that only damages you and does you no amount of good."

But I don't want to be an outcast of society! I don't want to have to watch what I eat specifically for the rest of my life and dread eating at restaurants or at friends houses because I don't know what's in the food! I want to be normal! And all the doctors

141

at the hospital assured me they had cured me and that food has nothing to do with it.

Well, all the medical doctor's assurances were pointless, because I was still in massive pain and not recovering well at all. I knew I had to give Dr. Lundell's advice a complete and honest try.

But First Things First, We're Hungry!

We stopped at a Thai Restaurant for one last hurrah before making a plunge into the abyss of social exile and extreme dietary weirdness for the rest of our lives. That's what it felt like anyway. And that Thai food tasted sooo good. I ate a ton of it. I cleaned my plate. And then another plate. I thought I might pay for it in pain and bloating...but I couldn't resist! I was overwhelmed. And it was my last time. I dare you to try to resist eating the whole plate on your last night of Panang Curry in your entire life. It's no easy task! Especially in a weakened emotional state.

But that was it. After that meal I was done. I was going to follow my new doctor's orders to the T!

That night the whole family was gathering again for movie night. They loaded the countertop with Peanut M&M's, Regular M&M's, five varieties of microwave popcorn, cheddar, kettle corn, caramel corn, regular butter, the works. Then there was the massive Costco-size leftover pumpkin pie, and the maple frosting covered pound cake. Oh yeah, and of course a token small plate of carrots and celery which nobody touched.

All of it was off-limits for me, even the carrots and celery because raw hard veggies were still too tough on my system. Whatever! I don't need to eat that junk anyway! I already had my last hurrah. I'm just going to watch the movie...I'm not even hungry.

90 Minutes Later...

After sitting there immersed in the smell of caramel corn and candy, watching everyone chow down on all the 'goodies', I rationalized making my way to the kitchen for just a look to make sure there was nothing that had magically appeared that was legal for me to eat now. I was getting a bit hungry now after all, certainly there was something over there OK for me to eat.

Nope. Nothing. Bummer! Well, I haven't 'officially' started on the doctor's recommendations anyway, just one little bite of that amazing smelling maple covered pound cake isn't going to hurt any worse than the Thai food I already ate anyway, right?

Moments later a thin little slice of the gooey, sticky, mapley goodness had made its way into my hand and on its way to my mouth. Mmmmmmm. Sugar. Oooohh, that tastes good.

Hmmm, just one more little slice like that couldn't hurt. Mmmmm.

You know how the story goes from here I'm sure. Soon I was scraping the bottom of the popcorn bowl for the last of the caramel drippings. Pumpkin pie? You bet! Oh who cares anymore! Bring on the M&M's!! What? All the regular chocolate are gone? Oh whatever! One more night of peanuts isn't going to kill me. Well, maybe those are a bit crunchy for my weakened guts...nahhhh. Mmmmm...peanut M&M's. So crunchy, so peanutty, so...chocolaty.

It's a slippery slope. And I slid all the way down. I had a hunch I was setting myself up for some pain...but hunches can be so annoying sometimes, who needs 'em?

By the time I got to bed that night, my bowels were already locking up. Uh-oh! This may be a long night. I popped a couple pre-emptive Percocet, but it got worse.

I may have slept for an hour or so, but mostly I tossed and turned in agony. Starting about 2 AM everything I ate came rushing out my mouth in violent convulsions. Miserable!

Drained…emotionally and physically. I still had searing pain in my abdomen with every contraction. It was a fitful night. But I knew at that point I had to make a serious change. That pain and vomiting sealed the deal for me. There was no question in my mind the sugar and refined foods were harmful for me. I would be a total fool to keep believing the medical doctors after what I just experienced. I may be a fool, but I'm not a total fool!

After an entire day of nauseous weakness and fasting, I ate my newly prescribed food that next evening: Cooked, soft organic veggies, with organic meat. That night I didn't have any bloating or bowel pain so I didn't need any pain pills and I actually slept. Well, that's an improvement! But the next day still void of energy, life looked incredibly bleak. That day Abe accepted an invitation from my sister to go and stay with his cousins in Utah for a while, even until Christmas if needed. Nan desperately needed help, and I was much too weak to help. My sister's service saved us again.

Continued Depression

Alone in despairing thought, I desperately needed some outlet. I wrote this in my journal:

Sunday November 25, 2012 – Thoughts on Life

It seems daily thoughts of death are on my mind lately. I find myself silently wishing I were dead instead of still here on this miserable plane of existence. How is it that my view on life can be so drastically different some moments than others. I must be experiencing some level of depression and hopelessness. The thoughts of wanting to die are so opposite of my deeply held belief that this is a truly amazing life. How do I reconcile the two? Or how do I get rid of the thoughts of wanting death?

Lately I have been so challenged to see the good and the beautiful all around me. It has become so easy to see the difficult, the annoying, the frustrating, the painful, the challenging. And it has become increasingly difficult to direct my thoughts to the positive aspects of life and my situation. I wish I could say it were opposite of that, but that's the reality. So what can be done? What can I do? What will I do? Well, I'm going to start by making a list of all my frustrations and annoyances. Then I'm going to attempt to write a positive thing or two about each one.

Frustrations and Annoyances	Any Positive Things?
I stink and I lack energy to shower.	I am humbled by this situation. I am learning patience.
I'm grossed out every time I empty my ostomy bag. My output is all black for 2 days.	I'm grateful that I have an ostomy bag instead of burning.
My stomach hurts consistently.	My stomach doesn't hurt as bad as my butt used to hurt.
My appetite is very weak. Almost nothing sounds appetizing. I don't know what to cook or eat. I'm overwhelmed by my restricted diet.	I have the opportunity to learn to cook tons of healthy and delicious things.
I'm annoyed at all the	I'm grateful to have

supplements I'm now taking.	supplements and I'm hopeful that they will help me.
I'm still on an IV and completely dependent one month after surgery. Surgery didn't seem to solve my diet issues; apparently I have dietary limitations regardless of my colon.	I'm grateful for the IV nutrition that is giving me nutrients in this time of recovery.
I am not able to be the parent I want to be.	I'm gaining such a deep desire to be a good parent. I will be a better parent than ever once I'm recovered.
I can't run, I can hardly walk.	I'm gaining a much deeper appreciation for health and vitality.
I want food but I lack energy to make it and I don't even know what I can eat that won't make me sick or bloated. I'm kind of MAD that I can't eat the things I used to eat, like waffles, pancakes, cereal, yogurt, cheese.	By learning to eat more healthy I will live a longer more healthy, good feeling life. I will be blessed by learning to eat what is nutritious rather that just what is easy and tastes good.

What do I have that's amazing? What is so worth living for?

My beautiful wife Nan and four amazing children. God has so richly blessed me with these relationships that are eternal. I want to be here to love them, serve them, and enjoy this life with them until I am old.

There is so much life yet to experience! So many places to go and things to see and do. I want to learn to surf. I want to see the world with my family.

There are so many people here on earth for me to serve and bless. I feel that I have a message to share and a light to give and service to give to the world. It would be a shame and a loss if I didn't share hope, goodness, and light and inspiration with millions of people. There is so much good to be done, and I can be an instrument in that. I want to be healthy and well in order to do that.

"It appeared the night may never end, and pain may last forever. But writing drew the truth from within and acted as a lever. It pried me from the grasp of fear, and overwhelmed despair. It lifted me; it comforted, and filled life with fresh air."

I just wrote that little poem for you ;) I guess I was in 'poem mode' as I recalled William Ernest Henley's immortal poem 'Invictus'. It has become a part of my soul and he spoke my feelings best. It gives me courage consistently in dark times. The truth of the last two lines could not be more empowering, especially knowing he wrote it while recovering from leg amputation from tuberculosis.

Invictus

Out of the night that covers me,
Black as the Pit from pole to pole,
I thank whatever gods may be
For my unconquerable soul.

In the fell clutch of circumstance
I have not winced nor cried aloud.
Under the bludgeonings of chance
My head is bloody, but unbowed.

Beyond this place of wrath and tears
Looms but the Horror of the shade,
And yet the menace of the years
Finds and shall find me unafraid.

It matters not how strait the gate,
How charged with punishments the scroll,
I am the master of my fate:
I am the captain of my soul.

Miraculous Healing

From that day on, all the bloating, all the bowel cramping pain, and all the toxic burps and gas were gone. And they never came back. I had changed my diet in strict adherence to Dr. Lundell's recommendation, and all the pain went away over night. Is this real? Is this a dream? Why didn't this diet stuff work before?

I had asked Dr. Lundell why the diet changes didn't work for me the first time I tried them. He said my body was in such a state of attack that no drugs or dietary changes could stop the momentum and destruction of the disease at that moment. There were so many antibodies created for my colon cells and my immune system was so compromised that the drugs and dietary changes at that point were like trying to dam up a rushing river with a couple sandbags.

Now with my immune system no longer in full-on attack mode on my colon, my body responded immediately to the change in diet.

And that changed everything for me. The next day, my energy came back and gained momentum fast. Soon I was up and around the house. I spent that week shopping, and cooking, and re-stocking our pantry. And I was fully onboard with the new regime. As hard as it was going to be and as much of an outcast from normal society it would make me, there was no going back to my old way of eating. The evidence was way too personal and way too obvious. When I eat poorly I have pain, disease, and potential death. When I eat well I feel good, I have energy, and my body recovers.

This seems so obvious, and it is. But why were all the medical doctors so vehemently opposed to the idea? I could postulate for a while, but I'll let you draw your own conclusions. Suffice it to say, I'm getting most of my advice from Dr. Lundell, and others like him, in the future.

It felt so good to finally see legitimate answers and solutions to my issues. Such a relief to see results! I now deeply empathize with those who are living with undiagnosed and/or untreatable pain. The feelings of helplessness and despair can be overpowering at times. But I know from experience that joy can be found in the midst of it all. There is meaning to be found in everything. Seeking joy and meaning, and trusting in our Creator's infinite love and desire for our well-being, allows us to bridge the gap of despair and to "against hope, believe in hope" as Abraham the prophet did (Romans 4:18).

Permanent Hope Returns

I wrote this in my journal two days later:

November 27, 2012 – How am I feeling?

Thankfully, the despair and depression I was feeling on Friday thru Sunday has lifted dramatically. My desire and appetite for food has gone way up. And I went to Vitamin Cottage with Nan and picked up a bunch of organic foods to start cooking with. Also, we got a Vitamix blender that is awesome and will definitely be used daily from now on. This morning I blended up beets, kale, chard, celery, carrots, ginger and parsley into a hot beverage. It was kind of nasty – but I got down 8 ounces of it and I'm sure that will be very nutritious for me. I also made a delicious guacamole with chicken blended in that was awesome.

Then a few days later I wrote this on Facebook:

November 30, 2012

Whoa! So much has changed in the 4 months since Kelsie's birth. We were all so happy and we didn't have any problems in the world. That day was one of the most intense days of Nan and my lives, yet it turned out so well, and our joy was overflowing. This picture is indicative of how our life was, in general. We were superbly happy. We had fun together, laughed, played, and had very few if any challenges with our kids. Nan was obviously challenged and uncomfortable with the pregnancy, but otherwise life was pretty blissful this year.

As I looked back at this picture just now, I could not help feeling a bit of grief at the loss of what we had then. Starting the very next day I began experiencing pain and it seems like the forces of nature have just pummeled us almost daily for four months. It has been so taxing on Nan, the kids and me. Our whole family has had to deal with fear, pain, emotional distress, so many challenges. Our kids are not the same. We are not the same. We have not had the same happy times as we had in the past for months. It has been a trying, and difficult 4 months to say the least.

But even though I feel some grief for the loss of what we had, mostly this picture gives me hope. My body is recovering and getting stronger every day. I'm up to 147 pounds from my low point of 128 a couple weeks ago. I'm eating consistently now and dialing in a diet that should work for me long term. I'm home with my family. I feel like I'm returning to my old self of being a happy, fun, optimistic, supportive dad and husband a little more each day.

And so seeing this picture reminds me of what we can have again, because we had it before. It gives me hope that my children, Nan and I can all recover from the emotional and physical beat-downs we have all experienced. I'm confident we will all recover, and I predict we'll be happier and better off than ever before.

Rapid Recovery, Continued Challenges

My body suddenly began recovering amazingly fast, which filled my bucket of hope daily.

Meanwhile, the news from Utah was that Abe's emotions spiraled downward each day he was away from us. Nan and I were taking time to reconnect, unify and plan for how to best help Abe upon his return. But every night he begged us to bring him home, bawling uncontrollably, telling us he didn't want live if he couldn't come home immediately.

We desperately longed to hold him and comfort him. Many nights we cried together, agonizing over our son's pain, but still incapable of bringing him home. It was pure mercy and grace from God that my body finally began recovering so dramatically that week. Abe's healing though, was still hanging in the balance.

Sunday came and we thought he was improving until we received this text from my sister:

> **Nan Kennard (M   ): From** Ash:I'm very worried about Abe. He can only think of one think: suicide. He ate breakfast and he is safe. He hasn't gone anything to hurt himself, but his spirit has changed. He says he doesn't even want to go home anymore. His heart has died. I am not a psychiatrist. I don't know what else to do.
> Sun, Dec 2, 2012, 1:31 PM

After feeling the urge to bring him home for a couple of days, this text confirmed that it was time. It had helped us immensely to have some time to ourselves and give him some distance from us, but it was getting too intense for him. We felt we needed professional help and fast.

Then just a little while later we got another text:

> **Nan Kennard (M   ): Then**
>
> later she said: Okay. He's back. My kids were the solution this time. He's drinking hot chocolate and laughing with the kids now. Wish I were trained in child psychology...
> Sun, Dec 2, 2012, 1:31 PM

What a relief!! Believe me, you do not want to receive a text that your son's "heart has died". Not fun!! My sister's sacrifice was absolutely amazing. She had four young kids of her own and a foreign exchange student. But she made space in her life to watch over and protect Abe in his darkest hours.

The urgency of flying Abe home immediately had passed. He was safe and clearly not going to harm himself. He told my sister he just wouldn't eat so that he would die. That would last sometimes just until he was distracted by cheerful cousins, or at most until the next meal when he would forget his threat and devour the food with everyone else. He was safe enough, but we felt it was time to bring him home because his heart seemed to break a little more each day. Within two days we arranged with my other sister to bring him home to us. He was so happy to be home! And it was so good to see him happy.

Thankfully, in the 10 days of his absence my body had made amazing strides in recovery. When he left I could barely get off the couch, I was totally unfit for effective parenting. The day he got home I had moved back into sleeping in my own bed for the first time in months, I was completely off the IV nutrition and fluids and I was actually doing most of the cooking and food preparation. My energy had dramatically improved. I was working my way back into being the father my kids had known. My girls already responded wonderfully to the improvements.

Things had nearly normalized in our house. The environment Abe came back to was dramatically different than when he left. His dad no longer looked and acted like he was dying.

He also came back to a vastly different eating regime. We had completely restocked the pantry and removed nearly all processed foods, all sugar, and anything with wheat. The day Abe came home was a touching and a tender night. Abe seemed truly happy again for the first time in months. After dinner we spent nearly an hour sitting on the couch talking and crying together. It was our first real connection in months. I just held him in my arms and didn't want to let him go. He opened up and his true self shined vibrantly. I knew then that he was going to recover and grow stronger from the experience. Though I suspected it would still take time and professional help, it filled me with hope to see his bright personality.

But the subsequent days he still suffered emotional pain. His upper lip had a constant nervous twitch and his gaze was unfocused most of the time. What happened to our son? Will he ever be the same again?

No. This had definitely changed him permanently. But I still believed it would be a change for the best eventually. I held the vision of him I saw that night in my arms, and I tried to help Nan do the same. Here and there his true self re-emerged and reminded us he was still there. I believed we were all experiencing this trial for a good and valuable purpose. But it stung so bitterly to watch our son's suffering, far worse than suffering personally. At times it became very difficult to see past the present moment of depression and fear Abe was buried in. Maintaining hope required a higher perspective. We had to try to see him from God's view. We had to try to envision him developing into the strong, confident, happy man we knew he would become.

What happened to our happy life? The only possible way to cope was to trust in the promise that "**all things wherewith you have been afflicted shall work together for your good**" (D&C 98:3). Somehow everything was conspiring for our good. But there was no way to see how. We felt immersed in total darkness. It required 100% faith. I had no way of knowing whether Abe would ever be back to normal, and if I allowed myself to dwell on that it was torture. Especially when I remembered my own role in causing his distress, it was too much to bear. But attempting to comfort Nan helped pull me out of my own irrational thoughts of fear. I felt a deep sense of peace despite the turmoil of emotions. I felt certainty in my heart that somehow we would be restored. And that feeling gave me hope.

Rebuilding From Nothing?

I wrote this on my blog a few days after Abe came home:

TrulyAmazingLife.com
December 7, 2012
Rebuilding From Nothing??
In some ways perhaps I am rebuilding from nothing. But it's more accurate to say I'm Building On Everything!

Today I am a free man.

My home care nurse came over for the last time today and discharged me. She pulled the IV line out of my arm that I was using for nutrition and hydration support up until last week.

I put on my running clothes for the first time in nearly 3 months today. I've got some new accessories now though, I also strapped on my ostomy bag support belt (for the bag connected to my stomach to catch the waste since I don't have a large intestine anymore).

Then I stepped out into the gorgeous, sunny, crisp winter morning and I ran.

It felt amazing. Then my left knee hurt and I walked. Then I stopped to rub it out. Then I ran more. Then I cried uncontrollably as I kept running; looking at the sun, and the sky, and the jet streams, and the flatirons, and feeling my heart pounding, and feeling so immensely blessed to be alive, and to be running, and to have excitement for life again.

My body is weak. I was able to do exactly ZERO pull-ups and ZERO push-ups today. And it took me 17 minutes to complete my one mile running loop. 4 months ago I ran a one mile race in 4 minutes and 37 seconds.

So am I starting from scratch? I could look it at like that...but I'm not going to. Sure I need to rebuild and re-strengthen my muscles and my heart and lungs need to start doing some work again. But I have a base of muscle memory, and knowledge, and experience that hasn't gone anywhere. All of which I am now building on. This 3 month break and the accompanied 35 pound reduction in weight I believe will turn out to benefit me as a runner. Less weight means less work on my legs, lungs, and heart after all. And my strength is coming back a lot faster than my weight, which only means good things as a runner.

So this morning marks the renewal of the pursuit of my goal of running a 4:20 mile and a 2:30 marathon. It will take time, but it feels so good to be working toward a goal again, and to have hope and excitement back in my life.

Emotionally, I'm building again also.

And so is my family.

The disease and surgery and debilitating pain I have gone through, and the near month I spent in the hospital, all combined to really attack me and my family emotionally. I found myself in the depths of despair and depression at times. It was the first time in my life I had experienced such intensely negative feelings and the desire to be dead. And I wasn't alone. My eight year old son slipped into emotional instability and depression needing to be pulled out of school while I was hospitalized.

And my poor wife was certainly not immune from the overwhelming anxiety and emotional challenges of having a newborn, a husband missing in action and fearing his death, and emotionally disturbed children to deal with. We have all been broken down and humbled to the extreme.

On October 27, the day of my emergency surgery, I was at risk of dying if I didn't have the diseased and destroyed colon removed quickly. And before surgery as I was screaming in pain, I kept asking the nurses if I was going to die. I didn't know what kind of pain meant death was imminent, and I was feeling constant, intense pain in my bowels.

But I desperately did NOT want to die.

Days and weeks later I found myself actually wishing I were dead at some moments. Not seeing any light to pursue. Feeling out of control from the pain, bloating, gas and need for pain pills and narcotics that were my daily companions. Feeling depressed about having to cancel our month-long planned trip to a beach house in Costa Rica in January. Depression and despair are not fun feelings I have come to learn.

But thankfully they have passed. Slowly, after weeks, the pain eased and I was able to go home. And slowly and with a lot of effort I am learning what to eat and not eat. And the result is I am no longer in pain. And I am gaining weight and strength little by little every week. And I am sleeping in my own bed again finally.

And I took my last pharmaceutical medication today, after a month-long tapering phase off the steroids I had been prescribed.

Today is the dawning of a new era.

Today I start to build on everything I have experienced.

And what an appropriate day, in Hawaii, December 7th marks the anniversary of the day in 1941 Pearl Harbor when they also started rebuilding.

My family and I have a lot of work to do physically, emotionally, spiritually, etc. But I believe all the work we are going to do is building on the foundation of experiences we have had. We are not starting over. We are building higher. We are getting stronger and will be better than ever before.

I can definitely say that I have more compassion and empathy now for people that are struggling in any way, especially with disease or depression. I have more knowledge of nutrition and health than I ever realized I would want or need to know. And I am so grateful to be excited about life again.

Discovering the truth about food set me free! Now I could focus on my family's freedom from the weight of emotional oppression still looming.

Chapter 9

A Fresh View. A New Life.

The New Deal

December became a month of growth, renewal, rebuilding, and recovery.

I spent hours each day shopping or teaching myself new ways to cook. Taking much needed naps, or going on super slow one mile runs which were so painful and yet so heavenly. It consumed multiple days to stock our entire house with new food products and get rid of the old. Do you realize how pervasive refined sugar is in our food supply? I was shocked to see it on the ingredient list of just about everything we had in the pantry and refrigerator. And the time required to prepare food and learn new ways to cook was enormous. But after what I had been through, I could no longer risk eating the same old way ever again. And I now knew too much to continue feeding my family a destructive diet. Ironically, like most Americans, we thought we were eating healthy.

Dr. Lundell and my subsequent life-enhancing experience with diet made it very clear to me that the diet I had grown up on played a significant role in causing ulcerative colitis for me. The medical community of doctors can deny all they want, and bury their heads in the sand, and just keep prescribing steroids and anti-inflammatory drugs for the rest of people's lives. But I don't buy it anymore. There are causes to auto-immune diseases. Everything has a cause. It's NOT just genetics as most doctors use as their copout. Diet is one of the major causes. It is certainly not the only factor. All stressors, whether environmental or emotional, play a role in digestive and auto-immune disorders. And genetic tendencies also play a role. But the diet we are subjected to these days, and which is common-place in America and many places in the world, is absolutely a major stressor on our systems. I cannot doubt that at all anymore after what I have experienced firsthand.

It became deeply important for me to create an environment of nutrition in my house that would support long-term health for me as well as my children. It was not enough for me to just change my diet and watch my family continue eating destructive foods and creating ticking time bombs in their digestive and immune systems. I could not justify contributing to that. And I could never bear to see my children suffer what I went through if I knew I had contributed to it through apathy. Not happening. Thankfully, Nan was convinced also. And the kids were convinced little by little. They had all seen what I had gone through, and now that we knew a large part of the cause was diet related, it was time we all made some significant changes.

It wasn't easy. In fact it was downright challenging. I hardly got any work done in my business in December, maybe an hour a day. And this after three months of virtually zero work. But my priority was healing, recovering, learning how to cook and eat, and focusing on helping my family do the same. Amazingly, my business prospered, and 2012 ended up being our most profitable year to date. And thankfully, our kids adapted quickly to the massive dietary shift, which was cool to watch. They did have their moments of tears over the loss of Life cereal and toast with jam. But that passed soon enough as they began enjoying new, healthier foods. Understanding the why behind what we were doing was critical for us all however, so we constantly reinforced that and taught them the truth about food (See the Epilogue for some reference material we discovered about healthy eating). Now we find our kids explaining to us how great it is that we changed our diets and why. It's very, very cool.

I was amazed most of all by how well Abe adapted to the new diet despite his emotional turmoil. But his pain was still a major issue.

Crazy Intense Tough Love

Abe often told us he was going to die somehow. "What are you going to do?" I would ask. "I'm just going to run into the street," he'd reply. This kind of dramatic discussion was highly alarming and often kept us hyper-focused on him. There were times he would throw a tantrum and run out of the house. We would go after him and carry him back inside, not knowing exactly how to react. Sometimes we placed him in timeout, other times we revoked privileges. And sometimes we just held him cried with him.

One day while Nan and Abe were picking the girls up from school, Abe got upset and crouched on the sidewalk with his head and knees tucked into his shirt like a turtle in its shell. Nan was nursing the baby while the girls played and Abe scooted himself out into the middle of the bus lane. Thankfully the buses had just left and it was empty. Nan scrambled to get him out of the street, but he stood up and said "see ya!" and bolted off down the street.

Holding our newborn, Nan was helpless to run after him, and quickly he was out of sight around the corner. Frantically she shuffled all three girls and loaded them into our white minivan to chase him down. She found him a quarter of a mile up the road nearing our street and asked him through the window where he was going. He screamed "I DON'T KNOW!" his face flushed red and sweating from running so hard. Then he took off back toward the school. She followed him in the van and he turned around again and ran the full quarter mile to our house. But he didn't stop. He kept on running past the house toward the busy street another few hundred yards away. Nan quickly parked and chased him down on foot, grabbed him tight in her arms, and carried him home.

She came in the door completely frazzled and scared out of her mind. They don't teach you how to handle this type of situation in "Parenting With Love and Logic"! Or were we just not listening? Well, even if they do teach this, parenting is a roller coaster and we were in for a ride!

Until now I was still hesitant to start disciplining Abe. I had so completely botched everything in the hospital six weeks earlier that I was clueless as to what approach to take. If I am strict, do I send him off the deep end and watch as he runs out into a busy street one day to end his life? If I am lenient will he spiral down further still? What the heck do I do??

Some nights Nan, as exhausted as she was from broken sleep with the newborn, had a hard time falling to sleep, not knowing if Abe would get up and run away in rebellion. It constantly tore her up inside. I think she has at least ten times more sensitivity and love than me and Abe's suffering was visibly taxing all resources. One night as Abe attempted to run out of the house Nan firmly stopped him and scolded him for even thinking about it. But then they both cried uncontrollably for an hour or so.

I was no longer willing to watch her go through the turmoil. A switch flipped in me that day and I knew I had to take control somehow, now that I had energy and some minor strength back. Abe was sick and Nan was suffering too. His behavior was unacceptable to me any longer. It was almost as if I had to make the choice between my wife and my son. It was torture, but I knew I had to seek Nan's well-being first.

We were beyond our wit's end as to what to do. With all the psychiatrist appointments at least three weeks out, our only other option if Abe decided to seriously endanger his life was the children's hospital ER. That was the last place we wanted to send him. From what we had learned, anti-depressants often have horrible side effects and can make things worse.

The next day we had a follow up appointment with Dr. Lundell and Abe refused to go. When I forced him out the door, he took off running up the sidewalk directly toward the busy street. I ran down the driveway in pursuit and he was already a couple hundred feet away, fortunately he had stopped to look back and see if he was being followed. WHEW! He was playing us. My heart rate had spiked when I thought he might be serious this time. I don't think I could have chased him down. But clearly he just wanted control and a reaction. And at that I realized that my Mr. Nice Guy approach was not helping him. I would not normally do this, and I don't condone this type of parenting style, but desperate times call for desperate measures.

I yelled in an intensely harsh, no-nonsense, drill sergeant tone, "ABRAHAM! GET BACK HERE RIGHT NOW!" He hesitated, and took a step toward me. "RUN!! NOW!!" I shouted. He started trotting back. Wow…it actually worked! That was unexpected. I thought I was going to have to blow my tough guy cover and ask Nan to chase him down. When he got back I commanded him in a very forceful tone to get into the car and in his seatbelt. He crawled into a heap on the floor and was bawling and wouldn't move. So I forcefully (with every ounce of my still limited strength) picked him up, put him in the chair, and strapped him in. He tried to take the buckle off and I mandated, "DO NOT TOUCH THAT BUCKLE!" His weak emotional state was no match for my firmness and intensity. I could not have done that a week earlier. He buried his head in his coat and just cried as loud as he could.

I was done with the manipulation. None of my niceness had been effective lately in the least. His despairing behavior only seemed to get worse. Plus it angered me to watch my wife suffer such intense emotional anguish every single day. I was done. And I made that very clear to him that morning.

I was extremely firm, but I don't think I was irrational or vindictive. My gut said this was the only possible path for progress. I could no longer stand by and watch my wife get thrown around on an emotional roller-coaster ride daily by this wonderful eight year old boy who was being controlled by his own fears and nightmares.

He cried the entire 30 minute drive to the appointment and then finally settled down. At the end of my visit with the doctor I asked his advice on healing my son. He recommended a couple of natural dietary supplements which he prescribed. He also recommended eliminating refined sugars from his diet completely, which we had already done. Dr. Lundell confirmed my belief regarding parenting, that firm limits enforced lovingly were critical. It was clear that Abe was feeling very unstable and insecure in life due to the crisis of my illness and surgery. He needed limits. He needed a firm, loving, present father and I was finally healthy enough to be able to provide that for him.

More Healing Miracles

Miraculously, Abe began transforming that very day.

He was obedient and respectful to everyone including himself the rest of that day. Not only did he not appear to hate me for the intensely harsh treatment he had received that morning, he acted with greater respect and love toward me the rest of that day.

He didn't fully recover that day; he needed time. But a major shift had taken place. He went for five days without any temper tantrums, screaming, or telling us he wanted to die! It confirmed loudly the importance of tough love and appropriate limits.

Now please don't take that to mean I condone drill sergeant parenting in a commanding and harsh way. That was an extreme circumstance where true love required that from me in that moment. It has never required that since.

Abe's emotional healing took a huge leap that day and it was a miracle to me. I could hardly believe it. Nan couldn't quite believe it yet, and understandably so. She had been living on a bed of pins and needles with him for so long that it took a couple weeks for her to fully accept the possibility that he was actually recovering. But by Christmas break Abe was back to his normal, happy self the majority of the time. He would sadden easily, but he no longer threw tantrums. And by Christmas, Nan and I were both able to relax, and fully feel the peace that had returned to our home.

Peace!! No more fear! Happy children that sleep in their own beds and don't throw tantrums all day! Our happy life was back. It was miraculous to us. We couldn't have asked for a better Christmas gift. Our son had returned; our family was reunited in love and harmony.

Regardless of Your Circumstances

A few days before Christmas, I wrote this on my blog as I contemplated what I had learned through this enormously trying season:

TrulyAmazingLife.com

December 20, 2012

Regardless of Your Circumstances…

We are all free to choose our thoughts, which control all of our experiences.

And regardless of our circumstances, we always have the freedom to choose the way we think.

Certainly outside circumstances, people, events etc. influence our thoughts and thinking. But ultimately it is up to us to decide what to think and how to think it. We get to decide whether to accept or reject a thought.

I battled with this concept a bit during the months when my body was fighting the intense battle with intestinal disease.

I had put my firm belief out there prior to getting sick, that This Is A Truly Amazing Life, and that we are all in control of our thoughts and thus we are all in control of our life experience.

And then one day all of a sudden, my body started breaking itself down for no apparent reason and became ravaged by disease. Over the course of 2 months, I lost over 50 pounds and ended up getting hauled off to the ER in an ambulance in the middle of the night to have an emergency surgery removal of my large intestine.

I would have likely died if I didn't get surgery that very day to remove it because it had perforated in multiple spots.

But before and after that day, as I suffered through months of debilitating daily intense pain, I was accosted with negative thoughts, and attacks on my previously promoted beliefs.

In April, when everything in life was smooth sailing, I had created this poster as a foundational reminder to myself of what things bring me true fulfillment. This poster became my daily reminder, and I now refer to it as the 12 Pillars of a Truly Amazing Life. I spent weeks pondering and writing on why it was that I was waking up each day so full of energy, life, excitement, and thrill to be alive. And these were the core reasons why for me.

But when my seemingly healthy body got overtaken by pain and disease, I was no longer waking up each day absolutely thrilled. In fact, I was rarely going to sleep the pain was so intense most nights.

Everything had changed again.

(To order an 18x24" copy of the Truly Amazing Life Poster go to TrulyAmazingLife.com/tal-poster)

There were a couple moments when I wanted to tear this poster off my wall and rip it in half. In those moments I could only see my pain and how my life pretty much sucked. How could this all be true? How could I think that life is truly amazing when I'm suffering daily with intense pain that I didn't even know the cause of? And how can I help others improve their lives by helping them see we are in control of our thoughts when I feel like I am floundering and completely out of control of anything??

My circumstances went from really awesome to horrendously nightmarish almost overnight.

And I couldn't see how I had any control over that. And I certainly didn't have any conscious control over it. Now that I understand the cause better, I can see how I did indeed play a part in the cause, but not intentionally of course...and that's a topic for another time.

But not feeling in control of anything, I seriously doubted those previously firm beliefs, and literally every part of that poster and my beliefs was put to the extreme test.

*And here are the results of those tests: **It's all true.** I don't care what your circumstances are. Nobody controls your thoughts except you. I found out that even in the midst of severe, intense, unrelenting pain, I still had free will to think however I chose to think. I could choose to see the pain as bad for me, or good for me. I could choose to focus my attention on the pain and the incredibly difficult circumstances, or I could choose to focus my attention on the potential good that may come of the experience.*

Nobody could force me one way or the other.

The circumstances certainly influenced me to focus on how horrible life was and how unfair everything was. But even though I was bombarded with those thoughts constantly, there was always another thought possible. There was always a positive side to every single thought and circumstance.

I can affirm now from a place of greater experience, that this is indeed a Truly Amazing Life. And believing that, and doing the other 11 things outlined on that poster, are absolutely possible regardless of one's circumstances.

Regardless of your circumstances you absolutely can choose to Believe that This Is A Truly Amazing Life and live it that way. Regardless of your circumstances, you can Celebrate Life, Smile, Enjoy and find meaning in this moment, Choose your thoughts and Create your life experience, Succeed, Remember who you are, Empower others, Give of yourself, Grow, and Love unconditionally.

All of those things are possible no matter what circumstances you find yourself in.

And I submit that becoming the person who naturally does those things is the most fulfilling way to live life.

This is just one example, but regardless of your circumstances you can absolutely smile. Well, I guess if you had severe facial damage you would have a hard time with that one temporarily, but even then you can smile with your eyes, heart, and thoughts.

And believe me - I understand how completely challenging this is when you are suffering with despair, depression, and severe pain. I have been there. And I completely failed to smile sometimes, even though I knew it would help me. It can be very hard.

But other times I succeeded. And it made a massive difference in my life in that moment when despite all hell breaking lose against me, I smiled anyway. It was incredibly empowering, and brought me joy in moments that would have otherwise been consumed by despair.

So Smile! You will be amazed at the result of what that physical action will enable in your mind. And even better than just smiling...look in the mirror and smile. No matter what you are going through, I guarantee you will be better off for doing

171

that. And you absolutely can do it regardless of your circumstances. And while you're looking in the mirror anyway, remind yourself of who you are. And say I love you to yourself and tell yourself why. You will be amazed at how much your emotions will change and improve by doing that.

If you need more proof that you can do these 12 things regardless of your circumstances, go read "Man's Search For Meaning" by Victor Frankl. It's a wonderful and completely inspirational book. His experiences of years of suffering in Nazi concentration camps were exponentially worse than anything I have gone through, and he was able to find joy and meaning throughout his horrendous experiences in those camps. And actually, the reason he survived was principally because he sought to find meaning, purpose, and joy in all of his circumstances, rather than allowing himself to think thoughts of defeat.

Regardless of our Circumstances, This Is A Truly Amazing Life! Believe it! It's true.

P.S. – I am running every day now. I've gained over 10 pounds in the last couple weeks, almost up to 160. Every day I'm gaining strength as well as passion and excitement for life. The last few months were insanely challenging and trying, but I'm thrilled to report that I'm back to being able to be a husband and a dad again. And what makes me happier than anything is that my 8 year old son has recovered immensely in the last week and a half and appears to be back to his sensitive, fun, excited-about-life, pre-emotional breakdown self. And it's amazing how much more things I feel gratitude in my heart for these days than ever before.

Banana Pancake Heaven

The entire Christmas break was pure heaven. Our life was back! Our family was back together! Two weeks like this: playing with the kids all day, enjoying delicious meals together, cuddling on the couch watching movies, playing strategy games with my son, watching him smile, laughing together, having tickle wars, Nan's mom staying with us for a week, thoroughly enjoying her company and help, taking the older kids skiing while Mom lovingly watched our baby Kelsie all day.

Those two weeks the kids were out of school were so precious and rejuvenating. It was like we hadn't seen each other for months and we were all getting re-acquainted. And we were in love! We had missed each other deeply, and it was absolutely amazing to be back in each other's arms, and back to laughing and loving together as an entire family. No schedules to keep. I didn't work at all. It was like living Jack Johnson's song *Banana Pancakes*, "When the whole world fits inside of your arms, do you really need to pay attention to the alarm? Wake up slow. Mmmmmm...wake up slow". I had envisioned this winter break living just like this in a beach house together in Costa Rica. We even had flights scheduled and a house there rented. Well, Costa Rica didn't work out, but we lived the experience anyway. We all slept in every day, and the kids would roll into our room giggling and crawl in our bed to cuddle us awake to make breakfast; such an amazing, peaceful, pain-free, happy time. Thank you, God! Thank you for healing us!!

The Human Body Is Amazing

I am still in awe and overcome with gratitude at the miraculous healing that happened in our family in December 2012. Though I watched it and lived its unfolding, I can't explain how it happened.

A season of easy happiness had returned. Smiling became effortless, constant and automatic again. I wrote this on my blog on New Year's Day:

TrulyAmazingLife.com

January 1, 2013

The Human Body is Amazing

8 weeks ago my body was about 50 pounds underweight at 129 lbs.

All my muscles were severely atrophied.

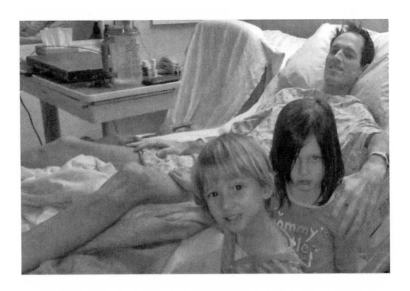

It was intensely taxing to walk a few feet down the hall in the hospital. I had to lay down sweating and panting from the exertion after.

At the beginning of December, I began watching daily in awe as my muscles came back to life and my legs visibly grew each day.

I now weigh 161 pounds.

Today I ran/hiked 12 miles round trip with 2500 feet of vertical gain to the top of Green Mountain and back via Bear Canyon in Boulder.

It took just over 2 1/2 hours and I feel fine now. Legs are tired, but I still have plenty of energy.

175

I am simply amazed at how fast the body can heal and recover. It seems miraculous to me.

I am super grateful to have my life back. Words cannot express it well.

I absolutely love life!

I am so grateful to be capable of starting 2013 conquering a summit alongside my best friend, my wife Nan.

Welcome to 2013! It's going to be the best year yet.

P.S. This Is A Truly Amazing Life.

The View from Two Summits

From the top of Green Mountain, many snowcapped, ice covered summits beckoned to me. Many of Colorado's fourteen thousand foot peaks are visible from there. It is inspiring to see them stretch out for nearly 180 degrees of view. I will summit many of them in due time. Maybe not in the winter when they are so treacherous, but who knows!

Simultaneously, from my viewpoint atop my 'Mountain of Pain', what called to me was the mountain of giving love, inspiration, hope, and encouragement to the people close to me, and to the world at large, somehow or some way. I wanted to somehow be a giver of hope, love, encouragement and inspiration to my brothers and sisters all over this planet. I felt some unrest from the top of those summits. I felt that I could not be fully at peace with myself, knowing there is suffering across the globe that I can help ease in some way, unless I was striving and succeeding at making a difference in whatever ways I can.

That new mountain is also covered with snow and ice right now. The task seems daunting, fraught with challenges and obstacles. But frankly, that excites me. I would not take it on otherwise. I crave the challenge. And I believe I am up for it. I know that in time, I will summit that new peak. All I need to do is take one step at a time, because great things only come by small things repeated daily. I know that I can make a difference, help people, and give compassionate loving service to my brothers and sisters across the world if I am persistent and hold onto my vision of that peak without wavering. In time I know that summit can be reached also.

And from there I will look on to other distant peaks, taller, and more challenging still, that won't be visible until I'm standing at the new summit.

Life is pure adventure. Life is amazing!

Conclusion

So What?

Curing The Incurable

All the medical doctors told me there was no cure and that I would be plagued by this genetic chronic disease the rest of my life. One doctor told me the truth and set me free. I will be forever grateful to my friend George for referring me, and for Dr. Lundell for being a seeker of the truth. Now I am healed, though a little lighter in the internal organ department. But who needs a colon anyway? Not me obviously! I now take zero pharmaceutical medications and I feel as healthy as I have ever felt. I do have an ostomy bag, which I have chosen to view as a wonderful constant reminder to me of how precious life is. But as far as ulcerative colitis and Crohn's disease, I am free of any symptoms and I have a knowledge of how to avoid their recurrence, which is very empowering. The surgery obviously saved my life for which I'm immensely grateful. But it wasn't until I learned the truth about proper nutrition and immunology that I discovered the lasting solution.

Here is a progression of the transformation my body went through over a seven month period:

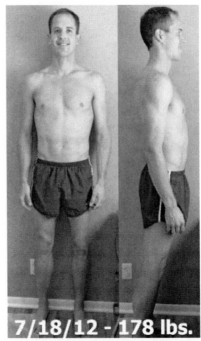

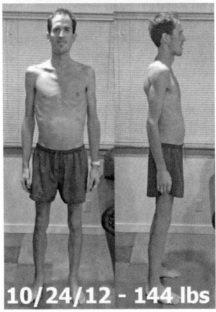

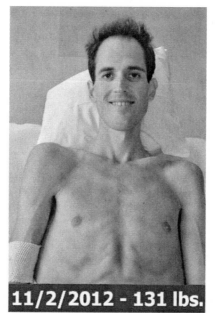

11/2/2012 - 131 lbs.

2/25/2013 - 172 lbs.

Oh, and here's the picture that started me taking pictures, long before I figured out just how truly amazing life was.

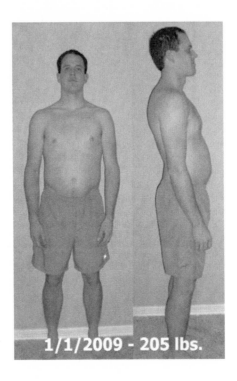

1/1/2009 - 205 lbs.

I hope my story has empowered you in some way, at the minimum by reminding you to be grateful for what you have. But I really hope that you believe that there is no bad day, and that everything is conspiring for your benefit. I know that to be true. And I know that truth will free anyone who embraces it fully just as it has freed me.

Do you feel empowered, hopeful, optimistic, freer, more alive, more faithful, and more joyful? I sincerely hope so. But allow me to close with some final thoughts, now that you have heard my story and we can relate better.

Are You Clear On The Secret?

Let me just be ultra-enormously-super-duper clear as we wrap up our time together. And don't be surprised when I repeat myself three times here pretty soon. It's important! I'm doing it on purpose!

Yes, I had many challenging days in 2012. We all have difficult days; it is part of life. And at the end of some of those days I wanted nothing more than to be asleep and out of pain for a moment. But I'm sure you are catching on by now that I don't have bad days anymore. And there was not one exception to that for me in 2012.

As challenging as some of those days were, I still knew deep within my core, that it was all happening for a good reason. Even while I didn't know how, I trusted that it was. And I still believe it, even though I still don't feel like I know all the ways it was good.

Ever since I made the decision to believe that **everything is conspiring for my benefit**, I have no longer had to wonder if some things are helping me and other things hurting me. I have no longer had to question every little thing and try to attach meaning to it. I don't have to wonder if I did something crazy to deserve this or any other question that used to pop into my mind when something seemed to go wrong in life.

I simply choose to keep believing it's all good for me, and somehow I'll make it through it, and everything will be fine. In fact, better than fine. Because all the hard situations I experience will only make me stronger, better, wiser, more compassionate, and more loving. And I will only turn them somehow into a greater benefit to me and everyone around me.

That is the belief I choose to hold. And that belief makes life a joy to be living, regardless of the immediate circumstances. Sure, I love the easy circumstances and I'll take them whenever I can get them! And I am supremely grateful to be feeling healthy again and easily enjoying life in so many ways that were impossible when I was sick. But I am also immensely grateful for some of the most joyous, tender, sacred, and love-filled moments in my life so far that I experienced during those months I was sick. And I am also super grateful for my expanded capacity for joy, love, empathy, pleasure, and a host of other gifts this experience of intense pain has given me.

It is all good. It is all happening for your good. Embrace that. Embrace your challenges, your pain, and your trials. **Believe that everything is conspiring for your benefit**. It will absolutely change your perspective on life, which will change your life for the better this very moment. Living that belief is the source of immense joy and peace, and will bring you joy in all the seasons and circumstances of your life.

I am grateful to have gone through so many trying experiences, because they have given me a much greater capacity for joy, love, empathy, pleasure and a host of other gifts. And I'm grateful to be in a position to share these truths with you. I sincerely hope it blesses you and helps you experience greater joy in your life starting now.

Why Should You Believe There Is No Bad Day?

Because that is ultimate freedom.

When you believe everything is conspiring for your benefit you can overcome all obstacles.

You will almost certainly be faced at times with circumstances that seem impossible and even horrifying. But you will automatically smile inside, knowing that they are there for your good. And even though they may beat you down into submission, and you may become discouraged and even depressed by the lack of ability to see any end in sight, you will still know deep within that it is all for your good.

And that deep knowledge will be like an unquenchable spark deep inside you. Like a pilot light that will never go out, no matter how hard things get. Your belief in the inherent goodness of life will keep that spark alive, even as small as it may be, nearly smothered under the oppressive weight of your pain, or depression, or both. And you will hold onto the belief that all is working to your good, and there is no bad day, and the fact that this is so difficult only means that more amazing things are coming than you can possibly imagine.

By holding that belief, you in fact enable those amazing things to happen. By letting go of that belief you are extinguishing your faith. And without faith you are dead. You may be still breathing, walking, and eating, but spiritually you are dormant, and either dead or dying. When you believe that all is lost, you have lost your hope. And that is a false belief and a destroying belief **because all is never lost**. God is good. The universe and the infinite intelligence that you are, that created you and breathes life into you wants nothing but your joy; your infinite, expansive, fullness of joy. But if you decide to believe otherwise, you make it impossible to experience true joy, and you shut out the good that is begging to rush into your life.

Yes, it seems in those darkest hours that life is horrible. At those times you likely will see no possible way it could be good. I get that. I have been there, done that. I know all too bitterly how that feels.

But the truth will always set you free.

The truth is that you get to choose whether you'll look for and find the positive or negative in every single thing. The empowering choice is to decide there is no bad day. The truth is that God is Love. The truth is that you are loved, cared for, and understood by your creator beyond your ability to even comprehend unless you are immersed in the spirit of infinite intelligence that you come from. Physical comprehension can't understand it, only spiritual.

Why should you choose to believe everything is conspiring for your benefit?

Because that is the way you can experience a fullness of joy in life. That belief enables you to become, to have, and to do everything you most desire in life. The thing that happens when you believe that is that you now see and expect everything to conspire for your benefit. So in every circumstance, whether it appears negative or positive, whether you like it or not, you choose to focus on what good can become of it. And you will find the good! You always find what you're looking for and what you focus on. You just don't realize that much of the time you are just looking for what you don't want. Searching for it, seeking it out, and lo and behold, finding it! Just think of any time when you felt horrible. Now tell me, what were you looking for?

Of course you find what you don't want if you are looking for it with all your energy. So stop looking for it! Stop concerning yourself with what you don't want! The only thing that you should focus your energy on is what you do want. And then you will feel amazing. Sure you should acknowledge the things you don't want when they present themselves, I'm not saying to put blinders on. But when you see what you don't want, turn your back to it. Use it to help you further clarify what you do want, and then focus all your energy and attention on that.

And know that this is a good day. There is amazing goodness in every day regardless of what happens. Every single thing that happens can turn to your ultimate benefit somehow. Just because you can't see that right now doesn't mean it is any less true. I love this statement by Albert Einstein, "There are only two ways to live your life. One is as though nothing is a miracle. The other is as though everything is a miracle." You are free to decide either way every day. Of course the latter is so much more enjoyable!

You Don't Need Smooth Waters To Be Happy!

I can't tell you that by believing and knowing that everything is conspiring for your benefit then everything will be smooth sailing and you'll never experience anything hard ever again. By no means is that the case. But I can tell you that by believing it you absolutely will be on the path to getting everything you truly desire and living a truly amazing life.

The challenge for some people is realizing and recognizing that sometimes, getting our truest desires requires us to pass through extremely difficult and challenging circumstances. Sometimes you can just be remodeled slightly. That's not super painful. But other times you need to be torn down and rebuilt entirely in order to become the person you need to be to achieve your heart's deep desires. For example, in a large developed city, in order to build a beautiful new building or structure, an existing structure needs torn down to the ground first; same with us sometimes. Yes, it is painful and hard to demolish the existing structure, but it is necessary in order to have the beautiful and the new.

In my own case, I know very clearly (and I could see it even going in because I was looking for it) that my experience with disease was an absolutely critical experience in allowing me to achieve my true desires. My desires were and are to serve and bless the lives of others in their time of need, and to do everything I can to make a significant and positive impact for good in people's lives with the time that I'm given on this planet. It is very clear to me that I am much more capable of doing that now than I could have possibly been without that experience. And I am truly grateful for the experience.

In your case it will be similar. By embracing the fact that every day is good, and that all things are good, you open yourself up to allowing the universe to give you everything you want. And instead of fighting and resisting and hating pain, and then suffering miserably when things that you don't understand happen, you embrace everything that is happening peacefully, and with gratitude, and grace. You look for and find the good in it all.

When you kick against hard things, it just hurts you. But when you see the hard things as beautiful, and perfectly timed for you, that is faith. And faith feels good. That is believing in what you can't necessarily see, but trusting in the hope that it is there. And by believing that, you actually cause it. **That is the creative power of faith**.

It can seem complex, but it is so simple! **Simply accept and believe that everything is conspiring for your benefit!!** That's it! Accept and believe that one thing and then you never have to ask the question again. You never have to question God's or the Universe's motives. The fact is they are always good and always wanting and desiring your best. God is pure love. There is a source of infinite, unconditional, pure love that is forgiving of everything you could possibly ever do "wrong" and wants nothing more than for you to simply love yourself and love others starting right now. Because you are infinitely loved, and because you decide to believe, instead of deny, the truth that everything is conspiring for your benefit, you allow all beneficial things to happen with ease. In denying that, you just push goodness and abundance away.

Why Not Get Mad?

I could easily have been intensely mad at God for allowing me to get that disease, couldn't I?

I mean, I had such big plans to serve others and bless lives through writing and teaching. And then all of a sudden, Wham! I'm on my back writhing in pain and nearly dying for months and almost completely incapable of doing any good for anybody. My plans completely thwarted and stopped dead in their tracks!

So shouldn't I have been ticked off?

I certainly could have chosen to feel that way. But in reality that would be absurd. The only logical and truly rational reaction to have, that is beneficial to me and to anyone else, is to TRUST! To have FAITH! To BELIEVE that "**ALL things shall work together for good**". That is the truth.

It is false to believe that God hates me and is out to get me and punish me. It is foolish to assume and believe that the universe is conspiring against me. It would be folly to believe and convince myself that just when I feel inspired and feel like things are working best, my plans always get shattered or halted by something. Sure, my best intentions and plans do quite often get shattered and halted and completely thwarted. But God's plans never do.

Do you think our creator just might know a little bit more than we do about what actually needs to happen in order for us to accomplish our desires?

Do you think He may have at least a slightly better perspective on it all than we do since He can actually see the end from the beginning all the time?

TRUST! When something happens that appears bad, just know that there is absolutely something amazing in it! Rejoice and count your blessings and look for how it will be good. Open yourself up to changing your thinking and your course if needed. Find a way around the obstacle. Make the challenge serve you! It is there for that specific purpose. *It always is.* There is a negative and positive side to literally everything. It's simply up to you to look for the positive instead of being sucked in by the negative and assuming that it's some kind of punishment or just a random circumstance.

Last Time I Ask, I Promise! (Today that is ☺!)

So one more time, why should you embrace the good day, and never choose to have a bad day ever again?

Because it's foolishness to have a bad day!

Yes, I know that sounds harsh. But choosing to view things as bad for you is either consciously or subconsciously deciding to be miserable and unhappy and invite more of what you don't want into your life. Can we all agree that is foolish? I don't mean to be rude to anyone by saying that. I personally have been in those shoes before and have been miserable and unhappy because I decided unconsciously to believe in bad days. But that was before I came to realize that it is all within my control.

Now that I know, I don't choose that anymore. And I hope to never make that choice again, ever. And I invite you to do the same. For your own sake, for the sake of your children or future children, your family, your friends, just decide right now that there is no bad day.

It is the way to be happy and to get everything you truly desire in life. It is the way to live in joy and peace. And that is my hope and my desire for you. You are now awake. You are now conscious to the fact that you can choose to never say 'I had a bad day." Now it is up to you. I have done my best to persuade, encourage, and provide examples and reasons. But the action and change is up to you. You must want it for you, and then you must make the change personally in your own thought habits. And most habits don't change overnight. It requires daily consistent effort to affect lasting change and create new habits. The good news is by reading this book you have already started the process of upgrading your beliefs, or in other words thought habits.

By Small And Simple Things

"By small and simple things are great things brought to pass; and small means in many instances doth confound the wise." (Alma 37:6, The Book of Mormon). That is a motto we would all benefit from living by in our lives. Habits can absolutely change, and pretty quickly too. But you have to do the simple daily work. By immersing yourself in these thoughts for 3 to 4 weeks, you can entirely change your habit of thinking and that will improve your life for the better forever.

Do this simple thing, and watch your life expand: Simply repeat the affirmation "This Is A Truly Amazing Life. Everything is conspiring for my benefit. There Is No Bad Day. " Repeat it as much as you can throughout the day, but at minimum in the morning, afternoon, and before bed for the next 30 days. You will then have a new permanent belief.

I want nothing more than to help you permanently change your thought habits so that you can live the truly amazing life that is already yours by birthright. I know that if you will diligently think these things daily for 30 days with feeling, you will absolutely create new habits of thinking that will enable you to live a truly amazing life. I know this because I have done it, and because scientific research has proven that habits are formed in that period time.

I'm actually so intent on helping you do this for yourself, that I've created a system called 5 Minute Mental Mastery in which I have made the process super simple. My biggest challenges in changing my own mental habits over the years have been:

1. Not knowing what to focus on and
2. Not doing it consistently for 30 days to create the habit.

For me, it took years to get my beliefs to the point where I constantly see life as Truly Amazing. I can help you shortcut that process. Go to 5MinuteMentalMastery.com and I will show you how. This system will hold your hand every day, for just 5 minutes, and give you the power and ability to permanently change your beliefs and habits.

I may not know you personally, but I believe we are connected spiritually. I love you, and I appreciate you for desiring to be better and improving yourself. We are all better when one of us is better. I believe in you. I believe in your capacity for joy, because I believe in us. I know that we are all inseparably connected and come from the same source of amazing goodness.

Make the decision today and make every day amazing!

Sincerely,

Aaron Kennard

TrulyAmazingLife.com

P.S. This really is a truly amazing life! ;)

Epilogue

Here are some notes for you on some of the things I learned about food as it relates to our physical health. Every time I share my story people seem most intrigued by what I learned about food, so I'll share that with you briefly here.

Sugar

Doctor Lundell told me on my first visit that 'sugar is poison'. This was by far the hardest thing for me to kick. It took me over a month to work up to being to stopping entirely. Sugar is in just about everything out there it seems and it is so addicting. I needed more ammo than just his advice, so he told me to read these books below. After reading, I'm now convinced and I was finally able to kick the sugar habit for good...I never eat refined sugar anymore. Until I deeply convinced myself of the truth of it, I struggled. It is so rampant in our society, and it is viewed as 'extreme' to not eat refined sugar compared to the 'normal' of what everyone is doing. But now I'm on board and it feels great.

And my family is on board too. Every time my kids avoid eating refined sugar they get to add an avocado pit to our 'party jar'. We have fun family parties or adventures each time we fill it up together. We don't force them not to eat sugar, we leave the choice up to them, but we are not shy about educating them on the effects refined sugar has on our bodies. And they're having fun with it. Just yesterday they were given Jolly Ranchers from their teacher at church, and my 4, 6 and 8 year old kids had a fantastic time smashing them to pulverized bits with a hammer on our driveway. Also, we have clearly seen improvement in their behavior as we have shifted away from refined sugars.

Sugar Blues – William Dufty

Written in the 1970's, this is nothing new. But the message is far from sticking in our society. We love our sugar! No matter how bad it's hurting us. And it's so easy to justify because everyone is doing it and has for centuries. Just read the book.

Sugar Shock – Connie Bennett and Stephen Sinatra

A great modern companion and enhancement to 'Sugar Blues'. Read it. You can overcome the sugar addiction, and it will enhance your life. If you don't think you're addicted, just try not to eat any sugar in any form for a week then tell me what you think. You're addicted. But you can overcome it.

Wheat

Wheat Belly – William Davis

Eye-opening information. I don't touch wheat anymore in any form. And not just because of the gluten, though that is a huge problem whether people want to admit it or not. My dad stopped eating wheat after reading "Wheat Belly" and lost over 60 pounds fast.

Genetically Modified Foods

Genetic Roulette – Jeffrey Smith – the movie

Genetic Roulette – the book

At least watch the movie. There are big potential problems eating genetically modified foods, and you won't feel it until it's too late (ask me how I know). Eat organic, good food. In my opinion it's not worth risking your life just apathetically eating anything in the grocery store and assuming it must be fine since they are selling it. Walking around with blinders on doesn't change the truth about what's really happening, though it may do a great job of convincing you it does.

Dairy

Many people are allergic to dairy. For me, this was hard to give up, because I love yogurt and cheese! But when I found out I am off the charts high on my dairy allergies, it became easy to never touch it again. All I can say is be cautious about dairy, and don't be surprised if you are allergic unknowingly, and if you find out later on it is damaging your body. If I were to eat dairy again, raw, straight from a healthy cow is the only way I would do it. The pasteurized, processed, nutrient stripped, then artificially pumped back up dairy in the stores today is highly problematic in my opinion. And don't be comforted by the 'organic' label. It's still pasteurized and problematic.

Read this, some great points are made:
Eat To Live – Dr. Joe Fuhrman

Some of the Best Diet Books I Recommend

I don't think there is one book about diet that is going to be absolutely perfect for every person. Every person has different allergies and has lived under such vastly different conditions. But these are the books that I know of and have used that teach the closest to the best general principles on eating healthy. Don't take this as a full endorsement of every recipe and everything said in each book, because they likely have some contradictions. But look for commonalities and seek to feel what is true and good for you. Also, take into account your own personal differences and body's needs. You may need some blood anti-body tests done to know specifically which foods your body reacts negatively to. Everyone is a little different.

The Maker's Diet – Jordan Rubin

Practical Paleo – Diane Sanfilipo

Well Fed – Melissa Joulwan

Doctor Recommendation

This is a tough one. Many people have wanted to see Dr. Lundell since I have shared this story. He is an amazing doctor. But unfortunately he's not in a position to be able to help the masses personally. There are only so many hours in the day, and at the time of this writing he is not even able to take on new clients. I feel incredibly fortunate to have gained entry before his doors closed.

But I know there must be many other doctors and practitioners out there with similar training and ability to heal and to recognize truth. Dr. Lundell recommended one place to start in finding someone who shares his views would be the institute for functional medicine. Their website is: www.functionalmedicine.org. I hope this site can help you find someone like Dr. Lundell if you or someone you know is suffering with an auto-immune disease and getting nowhere with the standard medical community approach of pharmaceutical drugs.

Your Next Steps

I hope you enjoyed this book and that you have made the decision to never have a bad day again.

If so, please do a few things right now …

1. **Leave a positive review of this book** by doing the following:

    a. Go to Amazon.com and search for this book

    b. Click the "Create your own review" button or link

    c. Give me 5 Stars and write what you liked most about the book!!

2. **Help spread The Positive Thinking Secret by "liking" TrulyAmazingLife.com on Facebook.** Just click this link: http://facebook.com/TrulyAmazingLife and then click that little "Like" Button.

3. **The MOST important thing: Join the Free Truly Amazing Life Community by clicking** TrulyAmazingLife.com and entering your Name and Email address.

    It is one thing to decide to change your beliefs. It is quite another thing to train your thought habits so that you can actually stick to that decision. I will help you do that.

My mission in life is to help you live a truly amazing life. That is only fully possible when you create the proper habits of thinking. The 5 Minute Mental Mastery system enables you to install new, permanent habits of thought through a simple action-oriented 5 minute daily teaching process.

Let us help you live a truly amazing life! It really is simple, and you can do it. Go to: TrulyAmazingLife.com

One Final Reminder

Check out the 18x24" Truly Amazing Life Poster at
TrulyAmazingLife.com/tal-poster.

This poster contains the 12 Pillars of a Truly Amazing Life. When you live these 12 pillars your life will be truly amazing. Use this poster as your anchor and guide. We will ship you a beautiful poster to hang in your office, room, or wherever you need inspiration.

CELEBRATE LIFE. HELP OTHERS EXPERIENCE JOY. YOUR JOY IS DIRECTLY PROPORTIANATE TO THE JOY YOU GIVE OTHERS.

EVERY MOMENT, BREATH, BITE OF FOOD, AND INTERACTION ARE A WONDERFUL GIFT. SMILE.

ENJOY. IT FEELS GOOD. IT IS CONTAGIOUS. IT WILL CHANGE THE WORLD.

THINKING IS THE SOURCE OF POWER. THINK

FAITH. FEEL JOY. DO GOOD.

CREATE YOU BECOME WHAT YOU THINK ABOUT.

THE LIFE YOU WANT. CREATE ART. LIVE ON YOUR OWN TERMS. THIS IS A TRULY AMAZING LIFE JOY IS THE FRUIT OF GOOD THOUGHT. IF YOU DON'T FEEL GOOD, CHANGE YOUR THOUGHTS.

SUCCEED RIGHT NOW. SUCCESS IS THE PROGRESSIVE REALIZATION OF A WORTHY GOAL. BY SMALL AND SIMPLE THINGS, ARE GREAT THINGS BROUGHT TO PASS. REMEMBER WHO YOU ARE. LOOK INTO YOUR EYES. YOU WILL SHED TEARS OF JOY, EACH TIME YOU REALIZE.

EMPOWER OTHERS. ASK THEM WHY; THE TRUTH WILL SET THEM FREE. GIVE

GROW. YOURSELF AWAY. SHARE YOUR GIFTS FREELY WITH THE WORLD; GIVING IS TRULY LIVING.

IF YOU'RE NOT GROWING YOU'RE DYING. LOVE UNCONDITIONALLY. SHOW COMPASSION. WHAT MATTERS MORE?

TrulyAmazingLife.com ©2012

Published By:

Truly Amazing Life, Inc.
4985 Moorhead Ave #3518
Boulder, CO 80305
Website: TrulyAmazingLife.com
E-Mail: support@trulyamazinglife.com